The Suicide Dilemma

A suicidal person perceives only two equally bad choices—living in emotional pain—or death. The person becomes ambivalent, unable to choose. It is this ambivalence that gives us the opportunity to offer other choices.

The Suicide Dilemma
Finding a Better Choice

Rebecca Morgan Gibson, LCSW
and
Lynn Mills

To Jimmy, Georgia & Veronica Huston and
Jeremy, Emily & Marcus Gibson for their
patience and loving support.

COSWORTH PUBLISHING
LOS ANGELES

Copyright ©2018 by Rebecca Morgan Gibson, LCSW and Lynn Mills
Revised 2023

All rights reserved. No part of this book may be reproduced in any manner whatever,
including information storage, or retrieval, in whole or in part
(except for brief quotations in critical articles or reviews),
without written permission from the publisher.

COSWORTH PUBLISHING

21545 Yucatan Avenue

Woodland Hills, CA 91364

www.cosworthpublishing.com

ISBN: 978-1-970022-33-9

www.suicidedilemma.com

Printed in the United States of America

Acknowledgements

We wish to thank the following friends and fellow professionals: Stephen Wolinski, Ph.D; Michael Berger, Ph.D; Lisa Holt, LCSW; Betty Aldecoa, Psy.D., MA; James B. Payton, MD.

In memory of Anna Harvey and Anthony J. Wisenberger, MD.

We would also like to acknowledge all the pioneering work in the field of suicidology on which this book is based.

This book does not contain psychotherapeutic opinions nor does it constitute psychotherapeutic treatment. The intent of the authors is only to offer basic information on the nature of suicide, and support in your efforts to help those who are suicidal. It is not meant to be a substitute for the advice of a professional psychotherapist. Always consult a physician, a psychotherapist, or a suicide prevention center when dealing with a suicidal person, as soon as you suspect the person could be suicidal. The authors and publisher assume no responsibility if you use the information contained in this book.

The authors have generally used male pronouns, but this should be considered to include females unless the context clearly indicates otherwise.

Table Of Contents

Introduction—
Can I Prevent Suicide?
    Anyone Can Save Another From Committing Suicide

Chapter One—
What Is True About Suicide?................................. 1
    The Myths About Suicide

Chapter Two—
How Can I Tell if a Person Is Suicidal?................ 5
    Situational, Behavioral, and Verbal Clues, and Symptoms of Depression

Chapter Three—
How Does a Person Become Suicidal?................ 23
    The Process and Stages of Becoming Suicidal

Chapter Four—
How Do I Know if the Person Is Serious? 37
    Guidelines For Determining the Person's Danger to Himself

Chapter Five—
How Do I Talk to the Suicidal Person?................. *51*
    Opening up Communication

Chapter Six—
How Have Others Reached Out? *81*
    Stories of People Who Have Reached Out
    and Saved Loved Ones from Suicide

Chapter Seven—
What Is Involved in Treating Suicidal People? .. *105*
    The Treatment and Recovery Process, and
    How You Can Help

Chapter Eight—
How Have Others Overcome Suicidal Episodes? .. *125*
    Interviews With People Who Were
    Suicidal at One Point in Their Lives:

    Ken—A man who felt like a failure on the job, jumped off the Golden Gate Bridge and miraculously survived. 126

    Dorothy and April—Dorothy is a mother who became suicidal while placing her daughter, who has a severe intellectual developmental disability (IDD), in an institution. Seventeen-year-old April, who is intellectually gifted, was affected by the family crisis. April first considered suicide when she was in the sixth grade....................136

    Ellen—A woman who considered suicide after the long-term illness and death of her first husband, her own bout with cancer, bankruptcy, and a divorce from her second husband. 149

Greg—A student who became disillusioned with the world and overwhelmed by the pressure of graduate school. 156

Chip—A high school athlete who became suicidal after a car accident left him a quadriplegic..160

Ben—An elderly man who became distraught and suicidal after finding his wife with another man...169

Peter—A man in his early thirties who became suicidal while fighting AIDS........................173

Chapter Nine—
What Is Most Important to Remember? *187*
    The Main Points of This Book

Chapter Ten—
What if a Person I Care About Kills Himself? ... *191*
    Survivors of Suicide

Selected Bibliography *195*

Introduction

Can I Prevent Suicide?

Anyone Can Save Another From Suicide

It's scary when someone you know is suicidal, and it's hard to know how to deal with it. You may wonder if the person is really serious. What do you say to him?

This book is intended to help you deal with this difficult situation. It is not meant to teach you how to counsel the suicidal person. Suicidal behavior is a symptom of serious psychological problems, and suicidal people should always get professional help immediately—but this book can help you handle your own fears knowledgeably and can teach you how to guide the suicidal person to the help he needs. The suicidal person may not be thinking clearly enough to realize he or she needs help, so it's up to you and people around the suicidal person—the significant others—to recognize the symptoms and take action.

The suicidal person wants you to help because it's likely he's ambivalent about killing himself—he may think he doesn't want to live, *but* he doesn't necessarily want to die. What he wants is to get out of an intolerable situation, and death appears to be the only escape. The majority of suicidal people send out verbal or behavioral clues that they are suicidal. These clues are desperate cries for help. You don't have to be a mental health professional to recognize that someone is suicidal. If you respond and reach out in a caring and intelligent manner, the person may be saved.

Suicidal people generally feel isolated and alienated—**breaking that isolation is the key to suicide prevention.** When the suicidal person withdraws from others, feelings of helplessness and hopelessness fester. His thinking becomes so distorted that he gradually comes to believe that suicide is the only way out. The suicidal person needs you to show him that he has other options.

Who Are These Significant Others?

Although this book is specifically addressed to significant others—the spouses, lovers, friends, parents, siblings, children, and other relatives of the suicidal person—it could be useful to the suicidal person as well. In many cases, suicidal people become frightened by their thoughts of self-destruction and seek psychiatric help on their own.

More often though, the suicidal person is not thinking clearly and needs someone else to help him. Everyone who is associated with the suicidal person is on the front lines in the battle against suicide. As Edwin S. Shneidman, PhD, a founder of the American Association of Suicidology (AAS) said, "The prevention of suicide is everybody's business." For example, co-workers who spend the whole day together are in a good position to notice when a fellow employee is troubled and possibly suicidal. They should notice erratic attendance, poor performance, and depression, among other clues.

Often, distressed children and teens put on a different, more honest face at school. School is an ideal place to teach suicide prevention and peer counseling. Teachers, school nurses, counselors, and athletic coaches should look for clues in schoolwork such as suicidal themes in writing or art assignments, as well as poor athletic performance, truancy, loss of interest in normal activities, depression, and behavior problems. Peers are important because they are usually the first ones—often the only ones—a suicidal young person goes to for help.

The elderly are generally more isolated than younger people. An elderly person's contact with the outside world may be limited, but neighbors, landlords, or employees of shops and restaurants that he frequents, could stop an elderly person from killing himself.

Professionals who come in contact with the suicidal person figure into suicide prevention as well. Lawyers become a part of the process when the suicidal person wants to draw up a will. The lawyer should pay attention to the context in which the client comes to him—whether he is depressed, distressed, anxious, distracted, etc. The same goes for insurance agents. Clergymen counseling a distressed person should not be afraid to directly ask if he is suicidal.

In many cases, symptoms of depression cause physical illnesses, prompting suicidal patients to visit their family doctors. Studies have found that three-quarters of the depressed visit their doctors shortly before attempting suicide. While treating the symptoms of the illness, the physician should be alert for signs of depression and suicidal thoughts. There have been incidences of people who have attempted suicide while hospitalized for physical issues.

How To Use This Book

If you merely *suspect* that the person you're concerned about is suicidal, read the chapters in order. However, if you've already picked up on suicidal clues and believe you need to take action immediately, you may want to skip ahead.

Chapter Four, "How Do I Know if the Person Is Serious?" will give you guidelines for determining how dangerous the person is to himself. The chapter tells you where to seek help in non-emergency situations and emergency information on what to do in case of a suicide attempt.

Then go on to Chapter Five, "How Do I Talk to the Suicidal Person?" to learn how to open communication with someone you are concerned about. The chapter contains sample dialogues to be used as guidelines for discussing your fears with the suicidal person. Chapter Six, "How Have Others

Reached Out?" consists of stories of five significant others who successfully reached out and saved the lives of suicidal loved ones. It can be helpful to see what others have done in your situation.

Chapter Seven, "What Is Involved in Treating Suicidal People?" will give you guidelines on choosing a treatment facility or therapist for the suicidal person. This chapter outlines what is involved in the treatment process and how you can help.

Once you've read those chapters, go back to the rest of the book. Chapter One, "What Is True About Suicide?" deals with the myths about suicide. Chapter Two, "How Can I Tell If A Person Is Suicidal?" gives you some of the clues suicidal people give out. Chapter Three, "How Does a Person Become Suicidal?" describes the process of becoming suicidal.

Chapter Eight, "How Have Others Overcome Suicidal Episodes?" contains interviews with people who were suicidal at one time, and will give you insight into how it feels to be suicidal. It might be helpful for the person you are concerned about to read this chapter and see that he's not alone—others have felt the same way, but have managed to get past their self-destructiveness. Chapter Nine, "What Is Most Important to Remember?" is a review of the main points of the book. Chapter Ten, "What If A Person I Care About Kills Himself?" deals with surviving another's suicide.

The information in this book generally holds true for all age groups, but there is additional information that specifically addresses young people and the elderly. Most of the stories contained in this book are based on real case histories or composites of case histories with details changed to protect identities.

A psychiatrist in the Midwest tells of one of his patients, a young man who was on his way to kill himself by driving into a concrete bridge on the local interstate. While stopped at a red light, he happened to glance over at the car next to him. The driver, a pretty young woman, smiled back warmly. As he continued on to the interstate, he rethought his decision to commit suicide. The young man figured that if that woman could give a complete stranger such a genuine smile, the world couldn't be all that bad. He decided to give life another chance, called a local psychiatrist, and made an appointment.

It's usually not that easy, but this story is here to help you realize that the suicidal person is often looking for any encouragement not to kill himself. He wants your help. By reaching out, you can give him hope—and ultimately could save his life.

One

What Is True About Suicide?

The Myths About Suicide

As has been stated in the introduction, it's frightening when someone you care about is suicidal. Learning the facts about suicide is the only way to combat your fears. Much of what people hear about suicide is misinformation. So, let's begin by destroying some very dangerous myths:

Myth 1: People who talk about killing themselves don't commit suicide.

This is the most dangerous myth of all. Eighty percent of the people who attempt suicide have given verbal or behavioral clues. These clues must never be ignored and should always be treated seriously.

Myth 2: Talking with the person about his suicidal thoughts or intentions will encourage him to do it.

Wrong—the exact opposite is true. Talking to the person about his feelings tends to lower the level of anxiety he is experiencing. Your interest and your willingness to listen shows your caring and concern. This is exactly what the suicidal person needs.

Myth 3: If I talk with the person, I might say the wrong thing and cause him to do it.

This is the greatest fear of people who find themselves dealing with someone who is suicidal and often makes them reluctant to get involved. The reality is this—as long as you are reaching out and not rejecting the suicidal person, there are few things you can say or do that will make the situation worse. By showing you care, you could greatly improve the situation.

Myth 4: Use reverse psychology—tell the person to go ahead and kill himself. He'll chicken out and not do it.

No! This is a myth perpetuated by movies and TV. It seems to work well on the screen with actors working from a script, but in real life it tells the person, "I don't care about you." It confirms the suicidal person's own belief that his life is worthless and that the situation is hopeless.

Myth 5: Suicidal people are "crazy."

They may be distressed, distraught, or depressed, but not "crazy." However, it is possible that a small percentage are psychotic (out of touch with reality) at the time of the suicide attempt.

Myth 6: People who use alcohol, opioids, or other substances don't kill themselves.

Abuse of alcohol, opioids, and suicide is sometimes called the trifecta that is causing a drop in life expectancy in the U.S. The percentage of problem drinkers and alcoholics among suicide victims is quite high. Some experts see substance abuse as a slow form of suicide. It's also likely that a person's inhibitions break down due to alcohol, giving him the courage to attempt suicide, or he becomes so drunk and confused, he doesn't realize what he's doing. In addition, people who don't normally drink often will do so shortly before killing themselves.

Myth 7: Suicidal people rarely ever seek medical attention.

Many people who attempt or commit suicide seek medical help in the year prior. Many of these people do report depression or anxiety to their physicians, but the warning signs of suicidal thoughts and feelings are often missed. The suicidal person may minimize his feelings and thoughts, or the health professional does not know how to assess for suicidality.

Myth 8: Only adolescents and young adults kill themselves in any great numbers.

While the suicide rates for adolescents and young adults has been rising alarmingly, in 2022 the highest suicide rate was among adults aged 85 plus. The second highest rate occurred in those aged 75 to 84. Some experts believe the number may be even higher because the elderly may commit suicide in subtle, unsuspected ways, by not eating or drinking enough, overdosing on prescribed medication, or having "accidents" that aren't actually accidents. However, suicide is the second leading cause of death for youth ages 10 to 24.

Myth 9: Children do not kill themselves.

Suicide among children under the age of twelve is rare, however, there has been an increase in suicide attempts and deaths among young children, ages 5 to 11. Adults may not believe that a child is capable of becoming depressed and suicidal. They don't recognize their distress, therefore suicide in children under twelve often appears to be impulsive. A five-year-old's suicide attempt—like suddenly running out into traffic—can appear to come out of the blue.

Myth 10: Women do not use violent means to kill

themselves.

Not true. Firearms are the most common method of suicide among both women and men.

Myth 11: The suicide rate climbs as the temperature drops. People kill themselves during the Christmas season more than any other time of the year.

There is a general drop in suicides around all holidays, including Christmas. The suicide rate is highest in spring.

Myth 12: Once suicidal, always suicidal. People who attempt suicide will think about killing themselves for the rest of their lives.

This is untrue. Most people are suicidal for a distinct period of time, once in their lives. The suicidal state itself—the period of time during which they might make an attempt—may last only minutes or hours. Only about ten to twenty percent of those who attempt suicide and fail will later kill themselves.

Myth 13: A person's decision to commit suicide is made rationally and logically, and is based on a realistic evaluation of his life situation.

People who are suicidal are not thinking clearly. They are in emotional pain and their outlook on life is extremely confused. They have difficulty objectively examining their lives, otherwise they would be able to see other options.

Myth 14: Suicidal people want to die. They are 100% suicidal and there is no turning back.

Exposing this myth is the heart of this book. Virtually all suicidal people are ambivalent about dying—they do not necessarily want to die, they just don't want to continue living in the situation they are in. They want someone to offer them hope and assist them in getting help.

Two

How Can I Tell If a Person Is Suicidal?

Situational, Behavioral, and Verbal Clues, and Symptoms of Depression

For three days, Carlos straightened up his normally sloppy room, putting things in order. He wrote a note saying, "Give back to John" and pinned it on a jacket he'd borrowed from a friend. It seemed a little strange, but his girlfriend Linda wasn't alarmed. In fact, his behavior seemed like an improvement.

When he asked her for a piece of rope, he stammered that he'd finally decided to get into shape and was going to jump rope as part of his fitness program. Linda thought nothing of it, because for those three days, Carlos had suddenly appeared happier than he had been in a long time. It was a relief to Carlos' family and friends. After years of depression over his brother's death and two suicide attempts, he unexpectedly seemed to be feeling much better.

Linda was unaware that she was witnessing classic suicidal behavior. One evening, Carlos used the jump rope to hang himself from the light fixture in his ceiling. Luckily, when he kicked over the chair he'd used to reach the fixture, his parents were home to hear the thump. They rushed into the room and saved him just in time.

Linda later said, "Now I can look back and see what he was trying to say with all those crazy things he did. You know, I believe Carlos thought he was practically screaming for help. He must have been really hurt when no one responded." With more than a little irony and sadness in her voice, she added, "Ain't hindsight wonderful?"

In many cases, the suicidal person's behavior can be simply baffling to those around him, but the suicidal person thinks he's being obvious. He can then feel hurt and let down when no one responds, and his suicidal feelings are reinforced.

Often, the suicidal person's message is too subtle for significant others to pick up on. Or they discount its importance and simply joke it away. "He'll snap out of it, it's just a phase," is one commonly expressed hope. Sometimes significant others doubt themselves and think that they are reading too much into the suicidal person's behavior. Or they dismiss the behavior as manipulative and believe the troubled person is simply seeking attention—which is true. Sometimes the behavior *is* manipulative and the person *is* seeking attention—in the hope of ultimately saving his own life.

Thanks to hindsight, we have learned the clues to look for in the suicidal person's behavior and what they mean. The most important thing to remember is that suicidal behavior is a cry for help. The suicidal person wants you to help him and will make a great effort to reach you. It is up to you to learn these signals and clues—the language of suicide—and know how to respond to them.

Situational Clues to Suicide

A person's life situation can be the first clue to suicide. Suicidal feelings are often precipitated by losses. In Carlos' case, for example, the loss was his brother's death. Keep in mind that it's not simply the experience of the loss, but the meaning which the person gives it. If the person you are concerned about is having a difficult time dealing with a significant loss—whether it's an economic loss, loss of a loved one, loss of health, or loss of his sense of self—be very alert for any suicidal behavior or verbal signals he might give.

Situational Losses

Love—Loss of a loved one could occur through death, divorce, the break up of a romance or friendship, or losing someone close through moving away. The loss of a parent through death and loss of family unity through divorce are cited as reasons behind many youth suicides. The risk of suicide increases if a death occurs in a marriage in which the surviving spouse is the more dependent one.

Economic—Economic loss might come through job loss, economic reversal, lengthy unemployment, loss of status, or retirement.

Health—Loss of health could mean becoming ill, becoming disabled, loss of sexual potency, or having to recover from an accident. Losing good health and mobility can be especially devastating for a normally active person, just as disfigurement by accident or surgery can be devastating for an appearance-conscious person. Sometimes just the fear of having a serious illness can make a person suicidal. There have been tragic stories of people who committed suicide fearing they were terminally ill with cancer or AIDs.

Sense of Self or Identity—Loss of sense of self or identity can be a component of all the other types of losses. A person may define himself almost solely in terms of his profession, a particular activity, or a relationship with another person. Losing that source of identity can produce a sense of confusion and is often tied into a loss of self-esteem. As he "picks up the pieces," the person questions who he is and the worth of his life before the loss, as well as his prospects after the loss. The loss of an ideal in which the person strongly believed can also result in a sense of betrayal and loss of identity. A person can experience disillusionment with religious, political, or philosophical beliefs, or a particular person. An example is a soldier doubting his patriotism when confronted with the ugliness of war.

Unique Situational Losses for Young People—For a teenager, a situational loss could be lower than expected grades or SAT scores, trouble with the law, perceived rejection by peers, or failure to live up to parents' expectations.

Be especially alert if the loss includes downward mobility for a man and loss of a love relationship for a woman. The greatest danger can occur when the loss is unexpected or sudden. An unanticipated loss can make the individual feel especially helpless and that his life is out of his control. A rapid succession of losses can also be dangerous. The individual may have been able to cope with one loss at a time, but taken one on top of another, he may become overwhelmed.

Younger people are vulnerable because it's likely they've had less experience dealing with a loss, so it may be harder for them to see themselves ever getting over it. Older people are vulnerable because of the sheer numbers of losses they may have experienced over a lifetime—death or divorce of a spouse, death of family members and friends, illness, unemployment, and retirement. Each of these losses in turn reduces his support network and because he's older, he may feel he has less opportunities and time to replace the losses. The more final the loss—particularly death—the higher the suicide risk.

Often, the desire to join a dead loved one is cited as the reason behind a suicide attempt. Losing a parent or close family member early in life increases the risk of suicide in a person, not just in childhood, but later in life as well.

Losing a loved one through suicide is an especially dangerous risk factor. A high number of suicide attempters have a relative who attempted or committed suicide. Even if a parent who is suicidal does not actually kill himself, his children may learn poor coping skills from him. In addition, the child must live with the continual threat of losing that parent. In many cases, in the instant information age we live in today, a peer's suicide can touch off a teenage suicide cluster. A teenager can be influenced by another's suicide even if he doesn't know the person or live nearby.

A very important question to ask yourself is—"Has this person suffered a loss that might be significant to him?" Sometimes a person suffers a loss that takes a considerable toll on his life, but does not appear to be significant to others. To many people, particularly the elderly, losing a pet cat or dog might be earth-shaking and even represent a final loss of love and caring. Or a teenager who is dropped by a girlfriend or boyfriend might suffer a tremendous loss of self-esteem, and even feel that he or she will never be loved. You must look at the situation from the troubled person's perspective.

Keep in mind that situational losses can sometimes be very subtle, and it may appear that the suicidal person has not experienced any loss whatsoever. In that case, the person may have suffered a loss that you don't know about, and recent experiences may trigger something in the past that he has never gotten over.

For some people, the fear of a loss is enough to cause them distress. Sometimes a person will anticipate that a certain loss is impending without any real evidence. For example, a person can convince himself that his wife is walking out on him, or that he's going to get fired from his job, or that he's got a serious disease—when in reality, he's made an incorrect assumption. The anxiety he experiences from the fear of a loss can be as great as the anxiety induced by an actual loss.

Sometimes a person experiences a normal change in his life which he interprets as a loss—a child leaving home, for example. If the parent or child lacks sufficient coping skills, both could develop problems. The parent might suffer from "empty nest syndrome," and the child may have trouble being on his own and handling adult pressures. A failure to properly adjust to normal changes in life can lead to depression, and possibly to suicidal feelings if unresolved.

For others, their suicidal feelings cannot be traced to a specific event, but to a general condition in their lives that causes a great deal of stress, such as difficulties at work or at home. One example is an adolescent growing up in a family beset with conflict, depression, and addiction. The child can develop low self-esteem and depression, which can lead to suicidal feelings. Issues affecting society at large—the instability in modern families, loss of the support network of the traditional extended family, discrimination (racial, gender identity, and other types), the threat of war, economic problems, and the increased pressures of the high tech, modern world—are also stress-causing conditions that can contribute to a person's suicidal depression.

Verbal and Behavioral Clues— The Language of Suicide

The American Association of Suicidology reports that in four out of five suicides, the victims give verbal or behavioral clues that they intend to kill themselves. Sometimes they give oblique hints that those around them don't understand, or blatant ones that are shocking, but are frequently ignored.

These signals range from saying outright, "I want to die, I'm going to kill myself," to quietly giving away valued possessions. Generally speaking, females tend to give out more clues than males do. Because of social conditioning, women are able to ask for help more easily than men. For example, young females are the most frequent callers to crisis and suicide prevention centers. The young tend to give more clues than the elderly.

Suicidal behaviors are the language of despair. The person can be saying, "I am in emotional distress. I have reached the point where I can no longer cope and see only one way out."

Verbal Clues

We've often heard people say, "I could kill myself," and perhaps have even made a similar statement ourselves. However, if a person begins to express these thoughts and feelings on a regular basis, it is a whole other ball game. People who talk about killing themselves often *do* kill themselves.

It is unfortunately just that simple. Any and all talk of suicide, or not wanting to live, or being better off dead, should be taken seriously.

Sometimes the statements are blatant:

"I'm going to kill myself."
"I want to die."
"I just don't want to go on living."
"I wish I were dead."

More often, the statements are subtle:

"Life has lost its meaning for me."

"I'm not sure why I go on living."
"Nobody cares about me anymore."
"Nobody needs me anymore."
"I'm not the person I used to be."
"My family would be better off without me."

Sometimes the statements are veiled threats:

"You won't be seeing me around anymore."
"You'll regret treating me this way."
"If you leave me, I'll make you sorry."

Sometimes the suicidal person will speak about his problem as though it is happening to someone else:

"I have this friend who is thinking about suicide."
"My friend has this problem..."

Teens will describe the way they feel as "down" or "depressed," or use profanity. They often employ special jargon verbally and electronically in texts and social media posts. The younger child is more likely to say he feels "unhappy."

Some suicidal teens put themselves down:

"I'm such a loser. I hate myself. I might as well do the world a favor and kill myself."
"Everybody hates me, no one will even notice I'm gone."

A younger child may say something like:

"I wish I was never born."
"I just want to go to sleep and never wake up."
"I want it to all go away."

Occasionally, a verbal cue will be accompanied by a symbolic gesture or behavior. For example, a young college student went to a Halloween party dressed as a skeleton and told people, "Soon I'll look just like this." Shortly after that, he killed himself.

Behavioral Clues

Unfortunately, not every suicidal person comes right out and says that he is thinking of killing himself. The suicidal person is more likely to give out subtle behavioral clues, some conscious and some unconscious.

Some suicidal behavior can be completely bizarre and confusing. For example, every day for a month, a very proper sixty-five year old woman, Madelyn, would get up every morning, dress, tie a little red string around her neck, and go about her daily business. Her husband and friends found this a little odd, but no one asked her, "Why?" After a month, Madelyn hanged herself.

Some suicidal behavior can appear normal in certain contexts, such as putting affairs in order, giving away possessions, and making out a will. It's expected for adults to periodically update their wills, but it is not normal for a depressed teenager to give away their prized possessions. These actions can be misinterpreted in the suicidal elderly since these are often the actions of the elderly who are not suicidal.

You must be alert to the circumstances in which it's being done. Is the person still active and involved in a variety of activities, or is this the person's sole obsession? If he exhibits other suicidal or depressive behaviors, he could be in danger. Lawyers should pay attention to the client's manner when meeting about wills. If he seems desperate, hurried, or anything other than business-like, he could be suicidal.

Behavioral clues are specific behaviors and can be symptoms of depression, especially for children and teenagers. (Depressive symptoms will be discussed later in this chapter.)

The first and most important behavioral clue is:

A Previous Suicide Attempt—A previous suicide attempt does not mean that the person will remain suicidal for the rest of his life, but it does mean that any future difficulties must be given special care and attention. After a person has crossed the line between thinking about suicide and actually attempting it, it's easier for him to consider suicide again if the situation hasn't improved. If the person feels guilty over making the initial attempt and distressed over failing, he may be all the more determined the next time. Also, the more severe his previous attempts, the higher the possibility of completing suicide in following attempts. It is best for the significant others to get involved in the treatment process and to stay involved until it is clear that the person's problems have been completely resolved. When a person has made a previous attempt, other suicidal signs must be treated very seriously.

Putting Affairs in Order—Some suicidal people begin to put their personal and business affairs in order, giving the impression that they are preparing for a long journey. If a person begins giving away valued possessions, making out a will, or planning his own funeral, pay attention. If the context in which he is doing this is appropriate, then there is no cause for concern. But if this comes after a significant loss or is an expression of depression and feelings of hopelessness, that is another matter.

The Sudden and Unexplained Recovery from a Severe Depression—Watch for any sudden mood change. Often, the suicidal person has been struggling with depression for quite some time and then suddenly has a lot of energy and may even express optimism about his situation. Remember, the key is the speed or suddenness of the change. People do not recover from a severe depression overnight. An abrupt mood swing may indicate that the person has made a decision and the inner conflict is now resolved. With this decision, the energy level increases and he may then have the strength to kill himself.

Obtaining Means for Suicide—Be alert if the suicidal person buys a gun, especially if he has never liked guns or wanted them in the house, of if he gathers a large collection of pills (both prescription and over-the-counter). This may be significant if the person does not have a medical need for them or if he is hiding them.

Composing a Suicide Note—A small number of people who kill themselves leave suicide notes. Often, people who have been prevented from killing themselves have written notes and left them where they could be found. This is a clear and unmistakable call for help. Do not ignore it.

Resigning From Organizations, Clubs, and Groups— The relatively sudden, unexplained withdrawal from social activities and support groups should be looked at very closely. For example, a person who has been active in his church, mosque, or synagogue for many years may suddenly lose interest and stop attending. Or a teenager who is normally an avid football player may drop out of athletics for no reason. This is often a sign of depression and could mean that the person is detaching himself from his environment, preparing for death.

Any Unexplained Changes in Behavioral Patterns— A man may begin crying for no apparent reason, a teetotaler may suddenly begin drinking, a normally placid child may become hyperactive, etc. Human beings change attitudes and behaviors in the course of their lives, but an abrupt change in behavior is a key signal to which you should always pay attention.

Symptoms of Depression

According to the National Institute of Mental Health (NIMH), fifteen percent of all people suffering from major depression of at least one-month duration, will ultimately kill themselves and it is likely that many more will attempt suicide. It is likely that 44% of those who have killed themselves suffered from clinical depression. One way to prevent suicide is by picking up on the signs of depression and getting the depressed person to professional help before he reaches the point of becoming suicidal.

Depression is very prevalent. NIMH has estimated that depressive disorders affect 11.5 million Americans each year. For many, this illness is severe enough to disrupt their lives. Women are more than twice as likely to suffer from depression as men. Depression rates are highest for people aged 25 to 44, and is rising in the "baby boomers."

While most suicidal people are depressed, a small number

of people do make impulsive suicide attempts. These impulsive attempts are less likely to be fatal because they are not planned.

The following are the most frequently noted symptoms of depression. If four of these symptoms persist for over two weeks, or if normal, everyday functioning is affected, the person may have a depressive disorder.

Feelings of Worthlessness and Hopelessness—This is demonstrated in many ways, either verbally or behaviorally. Neglecting one's appearance is one behavioral expression—there is sloppiness and then there is real sloppiness. While many teens might seem somewhat untidy, they usually take a great deal of care with their personal appearance and hygiene. Pay special attention to a person who has been reasonably neat throughout life and then either gradually or suddenly begins to change.

A person who allows people to "walk all over him" is also expressing feelings of low self-worth. He may also put himself down in front of others. Another symptom of low self-esteem is apathy or extremely passive behavior. When he is asked his opinion, the person will usually respond, "I don't care, it doesn't matter to me." He can feel so overwhelmed that he begins to shut down his feelings and cut himself off emotionally from others, until he has completely withdrawn.

Nearly everyone at one time or another has self-doubts and feels bad about himself. These times are usually brief and the person can eventually come to a place where he feels good about himself again. But if a person seems stuck in the "I'm not o.k." position, this can be a cause for concern. A danger is that he has been that way for so long, people just assume it is a personality trait and take this for granted about him. But, a person cannot be psychologically healthy without self-respect.

Physical Illnesses—Many physical illnesses are the body's responses to emotional problems. Though there are real physical complaints and symptoms of illness, there may appear to be no concrete, physical cause. This is a common symptom of depression in children. Some typical physical illnesses include head and stomach aches, high blood pressure, chronic pain, and irritable bowel syndrome.

Extreme Changes in Eating Habits—When depressed, people tend to either overeat or lose their appetites. While often treated as syndromes in and of themselves, eating disorders can be seen as symptoms of depression. Anorexia nervosa is the chronic loss of appetite, while bulimia is a condition in which a person eats constantly but vomits or uses laxatives to keep from gaining weight.

Interruption of Normal Sleeping Patterns—Over a two-week or longer period of time, if a person is experiencing oversleeping or insomnia, he could be depressed. A depressed person can sleep most of the day as he tries to escape his psychological pain. At the other end of the spectrum, the inability to sleep creates extreme fatigue, lowering the person's ability to cope. A depressed person may overdose accidentally on sleeping pills while trying to get some sleep.

Low Energy and Fatigue—Everybody experiences ebbs and flows of energy from time to time, depending on the intensity of their activities. But over a long period of time, if a person is getting enough sleep or even oversleeping, but consistently seems tired and run-down, it may be a symptom of depression.

Anhedonia—This is the loss of the ability to enjoy life, or experience happiness or pleasure. The person often loses his sense of humor completely, and may seem apathetic and continually bored. By cutting off his feelings, the person is attempting to escape his pain and distress. Unfortunately, it is almost impossible to cut off negative feelings without cutting off positive feelings as well.

The person exhibiting anhedonia no longer has interest in doing things that he once enjoyed. He may completely withdraw from social life. He may also lose his sex drive, which often causes a person to feel even worse about himself. Loss of sex drive is one symptom that prompts people to see the family doctor, hoping to find a physical cause.

Inability to Concentrate—The person may lose track of conversations and may not seem to really "be there" or think straight. In an adult, it can be detected in lowered job performance. In a student, it shows up in falling grades. In the case of an elderly person, others may mistakenly assume that he has dementia.

Persistent Sadness and Crying—The person who cries easily might begin crying constantly, while the person who rarely cries might begin to cry for seemingly no reason at all. Men who have never cried because "real men don't cry" may try to hide their tears and sadness. Crying as an expression of grief and sorrow is normal and healthy. It is even healthy to cry for possibly hours or days, off and on, after a significant loss. But for a person to continue to have crying spells for months and even years following a loss is a sign of unresolved grief and depression.

Irritability—Everyone gets irritable occasionally, but a depressed person may become consistently testy, even about trivial things. A danger is, after a while, other people may come to expect it and consider it a part of his personality. The key is whether the person is normally easygoing and if this irritability lasts a long time. A form of bipolar depression may be indicated by irritability and anger accompanied by mood changes (where the person goes from highly energetic to depressed).

Pessimism—This is another aspect which could simply be written off by others as a personality trait. But, if over a period of time a normally positive person becomes consistently negative and pessimistic about the future (especially when it is clearly unwarranted), he could be exhibiting a symptom of depression.

Preoccupation with Death—This could mean obsession with death or suicide. This is especially serious when accompanied by withdrawal from family, friends, and social life.

A Reminder—If you pick up on one clue, look for a cluster of clues. Do not ignore the individual signal, but don't hit the panic button until you have looked at the whole picture. If you feel unsure of yourself and think that you're reading too much into the situation, talk to others who know the person, and call a mental health professional. If the suicidal person really is sending out signals, he wants you to respond.

Substance Abuse, Depression, and Suicide

Research has shown there is a link between substance abuse, depression, and suicide. Many see substance abuse, among other self-destructive behaviors, as a form of slow suicide. Others see it as a way of hiding symptoms of depression or as an attempt to relieve emotional pain, and consequently, a way to avoid suicide. Termed "self-medicating" by professionals, the person is thought to be attempting to treat his own depression.

Another belief is that taking drugs or drinking itself causes depression. In addition, problems caused by substance abuse, such as disruption in relationships or careers, can compound the depression. Others believe substance abuse and suicidal depression are both triggered by the same underlying problems in an individual.

Overindulgence of alcohol can cause numerous problems in a person's life. Alcohol is involved in over a quarter of the suicides in America. An adult alcoholic is 120 times more likely to commit suicide than non-alcoholics. Alcohol can increase a person's impulsivity and decrease his inhibitions. Alcohol abuse can also increase negative self-image, depression, and social isolation. It can promote all-or-nothing thinking, which may result in the alcoholic coming to believe that suicide is the only choice in dealing with these situations.

Opioid and other prescription medications are now being recognized as being highly addictive and play a role in other serious mental health issues. In 2015, over 33,000 people died from opioids or heroin. Some opioids are routinely prescribed for people who have legitimate physical pain, most commonly

Oxycontin. Fentanyl is another powerful prescription opioid that is highly addictive.

Among the deaths from opioids there are unintended overdoses: however, many of these may be suicides. Use of opioids has led to an increase of suicide for both males and females. Approximately five million veterans are reported as being diagnosed with substance abuse and, specifically, opioid abuse.

Depression in the Elderly

Depression is common among the elderly, but is often overlooked. The symptoms, such as confusion, memory loss, and pessimism, may be misdiagnosed as part of some other physical illness, or written off as dementia, Alzheimer's disease, or simply part of getting old. One way to distinguish the difference is that dementia and Alzheimer's come on gradually (sometimes taking years), while depression comes on more rapidly.

Elderly people are at high risk of becoming depressed. As the body ages, changes in the brain cells and chemicals make them vulnerable to clinical depression. Depression is often part of many afflictions older people develop, including Parkinson's disease, arthritis, cancer, and Alzheimer's disease.

Often, the elderly are being treated by more than one physician because their general practitioner has referred them to one or more specialists. It is important to provide each physician with a complete list of medications because over time, the interaction between different medications might possibly cause confusion, memory problems, or depression. It is essential to periodically review medications and possibly make changes in dosages or eliminate some medications altogether.

Older people usually possess reduced physical and emotional strength, but have to deal with more stress due to an accumulation of significant losses. They need more support, but are at a time in life (due to retirement, deaths of contemporaries, or their children having grown up and moved out) in which they may experience greater isolation from others and reduced mobility. Some elderly people harbor an old fashioned stigma about mental illness which makes them reluctant to seek counseling. The important thing as a significant other is to remember that depression can be treated. Don't assume it's just part of growing old.

Depression in the Young

Young people, even children, can become seriously depressed. Children with one or more depressed parents are more likely to suffer depression as well. But, even if a gene making one more susceptible to developing depression has been passed down to the child, it's not inevitable that the child will develop depression. Depression is often a combination of genetic tendency and a learned behavior pattern, as well as a reaction to adverse life events..

It is rare for children under the age of ten to commit suicide, but there tends to be an increase in the rate of suicide in children ages ten to fourteen.

All children become sad and withdrawn from time to time, but the sadness can be easily lifted by a parent's hug or a special treat. The depressed child or teenager remains habitually sad and tearful even when there seems to be no logical reason for it. Depression over losses is natural, but when the depressed child talks about what a bad person he is, it may mean he's suicidal.

The depressed adolescent generally has very low self-esteem and is very self-critical. He may say that nobody likes him and that it's because he's unattractive or unlovable. He generally has overblown feelings of guilt and may feel responsible for things that are not his fault, like his parents' divorce or another person's illness or death.

The suicidally depressed young person may also become preoccupied with death and dying. The theme of suicide or death may run through his creative writing or art assignments, or social media posts. He may also talk in great detail about his funeral wishes. Children will often act out their feelings in the games they play, pretending that their dolls and stuffed animals commit suicide, or have funerals, for example.

Suicidal depression in the young may not be apparent. It is often masked by hyperactive, anti-social, aggressive or "acting out" behavior, or heavy use of alcohol and drugs. It may show up in accident-proneness or physical ailments for which there seem to be no cause, or "cutting" and other self-harm behaviors. If the depressed young person is withdrawn and not "acting out," his problem could be overlooked since he is not being troublesome.

Many parents have a hard time admitting that their son or daughter could be depressed or suicidal. The suicide attempt of a child who runs out into traffic or swallows household cleaners is often dismissed as an "accident." A child or teenager who shoots himself was "just playing." Adults will even deny blatantly suicidal acts such as hanging, saying the young person "didn't know what he was doing." **Do not dismiss suicidal behavior, gestures, or attempts in children and teenagers.** They may be young, but they do know what they are doing—they can get suicidal just like adults do.

The following are symptoms of depression and suicide unique to children and teens:

Problems in School—Falling grades, disruptive behavior, truancy, trouble with friends, or withdrawal from normal activities. School phobia may develop, in which the child fears going to school and will do anything to avoid it.

Rebelliousness—Unruly behavior, running away from home, or getting into trouble with police and/or other authority figures. An anti-social behavior problem, especially when combined with alcohol and drug use, is the most frequent risk factor for male adolescents.

Physical Problems—Illness, being accident-prone, overeating or not eating, neglect of appearance, disturbance of sleeping habits and, in the case of young children, frequent nightmares.

Emotional Problems—Self-criticism, preoccupation with death and dying, withdrawal, habitual sadness, and excessive crying.

Keep in mind that many symptoms of depression and suicidal behavior clues in children and teens can also be seen as part of adolescence and growing up, but do not ignore them if the symptoms persist or seem to be a reaction to situational losses.

Dyslexia, ADHD, and Other Learning Disabilities

Pay special attention if a child or teen has a learning disability such as dyslexia or ADHD—they are at greater risk for depression and suicide. They have a difficult time fitting into the world and may face accusations of laziness from teachers and parents, as well as ridicule from peers. Their problems at school with verbal instructions, reading, writing, math, organization, and/or social interactions can result in low self-esteem, frustration, and feelings of failure. Without intervention these feelings may escalate as the difficulty of schoolwork increases with each grade level.

Coping with a learning disability can be exhausting and stressful. It takes a lot of energy to focus attention on schoolwork and to keep up with the constant shifting of focus necessary throughout the average school day. Those with learning disabilities may feel "different" from other kids, so they expend a lot of effort in trying to hide their disability so they can fit in and appear "normal." This draining of energy can leave them feeling depleted and prone to depression.

One study found that about one-third of young people who died by suicide also had mental health problems, including learning disabilities. ADHD was nearly twice as common as depression for young children, and in older children, depression was over twice as common as ADHD.

It's important for parents and teachers to recognize a child's learning disability as early as possible, get the child help, and support them in learning coping strategies. It's also important to help the child to understand their differences and help them to see that many successful people have overcome their learning disabilities—and that they can, too.

Three

How Does a Person Become Suicidal?

The Process and Stages of Becoming Suicidal

In order for you to overcome your fears about suicide and to more readily reach out to the person in distress, it is essential to understand what the suicidal person may be going through on a personal level. This chapter deals with what the suicidal person is experiencing and how he perceives the world—and you, as the significant other. It also tells you how the very elements of suicide, particularly ambivalence, can be your allies in saving the person's life and getting him to the professional help he needs.

The path someone takes in becoming suicidal is unique to that person—but the attitudes, thoughts, and feelings he experiences are not. How did the suicidal person get into this state? It did not happen overnight. He has attempted to deal with the situation as best he could, but has been unsuccessful. As pioneer suicidologist Marv Miller, PhD has stated, "Suicide is the result of a long-term, gradual wearing-away process. What is being worn away is the ability to cope with stress, loss, and frustrations. (Suicidal people) have been nickeled and dimed to death in a psychological sense." They have needs that are not being met and attitudes that may prevent them from seeking help in a more productive manner.

Suicidologists have found that the suicidal person goes through several distinct stages: (1) he has suffered psychological pain, distress, and inner turmoil, (2) he has made attempts to deal with the situation, and (3) when his attempts fail, he begins to feel helpless and hopeless about himself and his situation.

Along with this comes "distorted thinking." He begins to interpret the world in essentially negative terms and may interpret past experiences as more negative than they actually were—even blaming himself for the outcome of events over which he has no control. He may also become overly-sensitive, magnifying a trivial situation and overreacting to it. The person focuses on the negative aspect of his own situation and begins to convince himself that he will never change the circumstances of his life or the way he feels. He now believes there is only one way out of the pain—suicide.

Maggie's Story

Maggie's family noticed a distinct change in her posture shortly after her marriage broke up. "She just seemed to droop. Her shoulders, her mouth, the way she spoke, the way she walked," says her mother.

Maggie describes her struggle with suicide in this way, "I felt like I was caught in a heavy, black spider web and there was no way to get through it; it just stuck to me and weighed me down." Others describe it as sinking into quicksand, or trying to walk in a straight line during an earthquake—the ground is shaky, their steps are uncertain. When her husband left, Maggie had lost part of her identity as well as her marriage, and was faced with redefining her entire life. Her whole world turned upside down. It had grown confusing, disjointed, and dangerous.

Maggie began acting differently in many ways. For about a month following the divorce, it took Maggie longer and longer to get up in the morning. Eventually, she couldn't get herself out of bed at all. "I just wanted to sleep for a few months and wake up and be through all the pain. The only way not to hurt was to be unconscious," she says.

At one time Maggie was active in working out, but she stopped going to the gym, saying that she didn't have the energy. Her lack of appetite made it even worse. When Maggie began saying things like life wasn't worth living, her mother became alarmed.

The end of a relationship can be emotionally wrenching no matter what the circumstances, but it can be especially devastating if it isn't one's choice, as in Maggie's case. The loss of control over her situation made her feel powerless. Combined with the emptiness and hurt from the loss of the relationship itself, she felt depressed and eventually, suicidal.

Psychological Pain and Inner Turmoil

Maggie and her husband had been having some trouble when he announced he was leaving her. She begged him to give it one last shot at making it work, and he agreed. Though Maggie felt her husband's acquiescence was halfhearted at best, she hoped against hope and put more energy into improving the relationship. Despite her efforts, a couple of months later, her husband moved out and filed for divorce. Maggie felt her world was coming apart. She coped as best she could for about a month, until she just couldn't anymore.

Every day, people experience devastating losses and don't become suicidal. Why are certain people overwhelmed? One contributing factor may be that they have inadequate coping skills. Coping skills are the ways in which people deal with their stress and feelings. They learn them from their families and from their life experiences. With positive coping skills, a person can deal with situations and move on with life.

Some positive coping skills include the ability to mourn losses completely, the ability to learn from mistakes without getting down on oneself, and the ability to accept and adapt to changes in life. An important coping skill that suicidal people often lack is the ability to effectively deal with anger—they have trouble understanding its usefulness and expressing it appropriately.

Besides lacking positive coping skills, suicidal people

will often exhibit negative coping skills, such as "perfectionism." Perfectionists are extremely self-critical and cannot tolerate the fact that they make mistakes. They experience a tremendous loss of self-esteem when faced with life's disappointments. They think, "If I'm perfect, bad things shouldn't happen to me. I'm not supposed to get depressed." Perfectionism can be a common problem for adolescents, who haven't had enough experience in learning from their mistakes and may view them as irrevocable catastrophes.

Coping strategies boil down to the person's attitudes toward his own feelings and emotions. A suicidal person is often trapped in negative thinking and attitudes, and is unable to enjoy life. He also tends to deny his emotions and keeps them bottled up inside himself. This can make him *feel* isolated and cut off from other people, whether he actually is or not. Suicide is the ultimate negative coping method, which he employs when all others are exhausted.

Attempting Solutions

As Maggie tells it, "I tried to work out at the gym. That always made me feel good before, but not anymore. I even indulged myself by taking a trip to Hawaii, my favorite place, but I couldn't even enjoy that. The fact that I was still miserable doing my favorite things made me feel even worse. There was nothing I could do to get away from the pain. Except sleep. Or die."

All losses require a period of grief and mourning during which they are felt deeply. During and following the divorce, Maggie suffered loss, rejection, and abandonment. Of course no one wants to feel pain, so she responded in a natural manner—she tried to escape from the feelings by sleeping a lot. Not only was sleeping a way to avoid dealing with her problems, she was physically and mentally exhausted by the struggle to resolve her problems.

When that didn't work, she tried methods that she had developed over the years to deal with emotional discomfort and anxiety. When her coping skills fell short and her emotional needs were not met, she began to focus on one sure way of escape—if the unconsciousness of sleep did not offer relief, maybe death would.

Situational Depression

Almost everyone experiences periods of sadness, which the average person refers to as "feeling depressed." For most people, these periods will be brief, lasting a few days, maybe a week, and do not seriously interfere with daily functioning. Also identified as feeling "burned out," "down," or "blue," these are part of the normal ups and downs that come with life. If you aren't down occasionally, you aren't paying attention.

Situational depression is a legitimate response to unwanted changes, stresses, or losses. People who have suffered a loss, especially a major loss, have the right and the need to feel bad as they adjust and reorganize their lives. Situational depression is characterized by both good days and bad days. Over a period of time, the person regroups, adjusts to the loss, and goes on with life. People with situational depression often need extra support and nurturing from family and friends. However, sometimes situational depression can develop into clinical depression.

Maggie became depressed over her divorce and as time went on, it grew worse. She felt depressed about being depressed, which created a vicious cycle. Since depression has for so long been considered a spiritual malady or a deficiency in character, many people feel bad about having this problem, and even worse about admitting it. Says Maggie, "I'd been raised to always be happy. But now I wasn't. Being depressed made me feel weak and selfish, like I couldn't handle my problems."

When Maggie got a raise in salary, she couldn't feel pleasure in it. A dedicated, dynamic career woman, she had worked her way up from secretary to an executive position of respect and authority, but she became detached. "I'd try to get into my work, figuring that was one way to get over all the personal stuff, but I couldn't concentrate. I couldn't think straight. Making decisions on the job was really difficult. I knew how ineffective I was becoming and that made me feel even worse. And my self-esteem was already shot by the divorce. I kept wishing I could put my job on hold and deal with my problems before I inflicted any more damage on my career. All I could think about was the divorce and how miserable I felt."

She began to think often of death—just vague ideas at first, like how much easier things would be if she'd die, perhaps in a plane crash when on a business trip. The daydreams mirrored the sense of inner death she had been feeling since the end of her marriage. They developed into thoughts of suicide which, at first, were useful in protecting her from her fears about the future and gave her a badly needed sense of control over her life. She could flirt with ending it, pull back, then get on with living. But as her situation failed to improve, her thoughts crossed the line of fantasy, and dying became a possible solution to her problems. The initial wispy visions of death solidified into clear-cut thoughts of suicide.

It is not unusual for a person experiencing a situational depression to have suicidal feelings. Sometimes, the depressed person can view his suicidal thoughts as signals that he needs help. Some people will enter therapy saying, "When I began having thoughts about suicide, I knew it was time to call for help."

To recover from situational depression, sometimes psychotherapy is sufficient and antidepressants are not needed. This therapy usually involves learning new coping skills and resolving bad feelings. For example, widows or widowers may harbor feelings of guilt and disloyalty when they are ready to get into new relationships and build new lives.

In Maggie's case, her divorce brought up unresolved feelings of anger and depression which she experienced over her parents' divorce when she was a young child. Dealing with these recalled fears of abandonment was necessary before she could go on with her life.

Clinical Depression

There is another category of depression—clinical depression—which is an emotional disorder involving biochemical changes that result in an imbalance in brain chemistry. A large number of suicidal people suffer this type of depression. According to the latest research, some people may have a genetic predisposition to biochemical imbalances which can cause situational depression to develop into clinical depression under certain stressful conditions. The clinical, biochemical depression affects not only the person's mood, but his thinking processes and behavior as well.

In brief, the brain has a communications network made up of many different systems, not unlike computer networks. Within the system are billions of neurons which send and receive a variety of messages. The messages are sent across the synapses—tiny gaps between nerve endings—through chemicals called neurotransmitters. Among other duties, neurotransmitters modulate pain, hunger, sleep, learning, and memory, in addition to affecting emotions, moods, and behavior. While there are many chemicals involved in this transmission process, three appear to play a particularly important role in the development of depression: norepinephrine, serotonin, and dopamine.

The neurotransmitters interact with hormones produced by the glands of the endocrine system. These glands (hypothalamus, thyroid, pituitary, adrenals, testes, and ovaries, to name a few), regulate all the body's functions, from emotions to heart rate. They keep the body in balance by secreting the proper level of hormone. This equilibrium can be thrown off if there is an imbalance in the neurotransmitters. Likewise, a hormone imbalance originating in the glands can set off an imbalance in the neurotransmitters. These imbalances in the neurotransmitters and hormones may result in a clinical depression.

For many people who develop clinical depression and become suicidal, there is not an obvious major event or series of events that you can point to as having caused it. These people may have been under varying degrees of stress for long periods of time, possibly years. If a person does not have adequate coping skills to manage these daily stressors effectively, the stress may overwhelm him, and he can become mentally, emotionally, and even physically exhausted. This, in turn, can bring on physiological changes in the body, and the person may develop clinical depression.

Clinical depression is almost always treated with antidepressants in conjunction with psychotherapy. It is a chemical disorder which cannot be wished away. Telling a chemically depressed person to "snap out of it" is like asking a diabetic to "snap out of it." Unfortunately, depression is a disorder that can recur multiple times in a person's life. The good news is that depression, either situational or clinical, is the most treatable disorder in mental health.

Bipolar Disorder

Bipolar disorder is a mental disorder marked by alternating periods of elation and depression. Bipolar disorder may affect as many as 60 million people worldwide. Most people with bipolar disorder begin seeing symptoms between the ages of 15 to 25.

In the past this was referred to as manic depression. Bipolar disorder is inherited, however not everyone in a family with the genetic trait will develop the disorder. There is no cure for bipolar disorder, however the symptoms can be controlled with treatment.

A manic episode may include euphoria, high productivity and joyousness, over-excitement, irregular sleep patterns (many people with bipolar disorder will be unable to sleep for days at a time), poor judgment, risky behaviors, impulsivity (spending sprees), talking fast, and racing thoughts (the inability to stop or slow down one's thinking).

The depressive episodes in bipolar disorder may include many of the symptoms of clinical depression. The person may feel down or sad and experience feelings of helplessness and hopelessness. He may sleep too much or too little, may feel like he can't enjoy anything, may feel worried and empty, and may talk about death or suicide. Both manic and depressive episodes may include irritability and anger for no apparent reason.

For many people with bipolar disorder, the shift in mood from mania to depression happens very quickly. Some have described it as feeling like they are falling off an emotional cliff. They report that when they are in a manic episode they are terrified of the drop into depression.

People with bipolar disorder tend to self-medicate with drugs or alcohol in an attempt to manage the mood swings.

Many will take stimulants in an attempt to maintain the high or manic phase of the cycle.

Bipolar disorder carries a high risk of suicide. While statistics vary, it is estimated that as many as fifteen percent of people with bipolar disorder will commit suicide. Many of these people will have made more than one attempt before killing themselves. People with bipolar disorder are at a higher risk of suicide when they are in the depressive phase, and the clues they exhibit, both verbal and behavioral, are often the same as those of a person with clinical depression.

It is important to note that depression in bipolar disorder is not treated the same way as clinical depression. Antidepressants are not recommended for the depressive phase of bipolar disorder.

Bipolar disorder cannot be cured, but it can be managed. Medications for bipolar disorder are referred to as mood stabilizers. The medication most often used and considered the most successful is lithium, which has been used to treat bipolar disorder for many years. In the past few years, other medications have proved to have some success. This category of mood stabilizers was originally developed to manage seizure disorders. The one used most often is Lamictal. Another new medication is Latuda, which has been approved to treat bipolar disorder in adults and has been proven effective in many people struggling with bipolar disorder.

At present, the most successful approach in managing bipolar disorder is a combination of psychotherapy focused on stress management and finding the medication that is most effective for that individual.

Distorted Thinking

As a person becomes more depressed, his view of the world becomes more distorted. He feels so bad about himself that he is sure others see him similarly even though, in reality, they may not have changed their feelings toward him. A depressed person can convince himself, for example, that his girlfriend no longer wants him and is about to walk out on him, even when he has nothing to base it on. He will then misinterpret everything his girlfriend does in order to prove his point and may create so much tension in the relationship that he drives his girlfriend away, fulfilling his expectation.

The depressed person may also become overly-sensitive and overreact to trivial situations. Little slights can be blown completely out of proportion. For example, suppose you're friendly to a stranger and he doesn't respond. The typical reaction is to shrug and forget it because it's obviously the stranger's problem. However, an experience like that can be crushing to a depressed person, reinforcing his negative self-image of himself.

A kind of paranoia can even set in. The suicidal person may assume he knows what others are thinking about him, and it's almost always negative. As Maggie tells it, a smile from a passerby would send her frantically checking to see if a button on her blouse was missing or if there was lipstick on her teeth. It didn't occur to her that the person was being friendly or polite. "I felt they were smiling because they had something on me," says Maggie.

"One time, when I was in the middle of this whole mess, my boss (a man) told me how well I'd done in a presentation. Looking back, I don't know what made me snap, but I said, very sarcastically, 'You mean not bad for a girl, right?' which isn't what he meant at all. But I took what he said as a backhanded compliment," remembers Maggie.

The person not only misinterprets the outside world, but also begins to see his own situation in distorted terms. As his coping skills fail and he slides deeper and deeper into despair, he begins to feel incapable of helping himself. No longer recognizing his own strengths, he begins to unconsciously expect others to rescue him. When this does not happen, he begins to feel that his luck has run out.

As Maggie began to feel she was running out of options to change her life, she developed a kind of tunnel vision. The only thing visible at the end of that tunnel was suicide. All the other possible options were blocked out.

This inability to perceive choices is the hallmark of suicidal thinking and a major characteristic of clinical depression.

For many reasons, the suicidal person may seem to reject people who are trying to help. Distorted thinking can cause him to misinterpret a significant other's reaching out. Maggie saw her mother's and friends' sincere efforts to help as criticism. As a significant other, you may be alarmed by the suicidal person's behavior and general outlook, and become quite frustrated in trying to reach out to him. Don't give up.

Another obstacle in the intervention process is that the suicidal person may feel like a failure and be embarrassed about appearing weak or needy. In addition, the person or object that is lost may be the only thing that he thinks will satisfy him. In the case of the break up of a relationship, the suicidal person might focus on the lost love object. He can become obsessed with the idea that restoring the relationship exactly as it was before is the only reason to live. Though the person cares about his family, friends, or co-workers, they just aren't enough.

Timing is critical as well. Maggie's mother suggested to her that she go into therapy at the beginning of the divorce proceedings, saying, "It might help you get through this better." Maggie scoffed at the idea, seeing herself as balanced enough to deal with it on her own. She also harbored a lot of denial. "Part of me thought it really wasn't going to happen, that one day my husband would see the light. I'd wake up and the marriage would work out somehow."

Even when she realized that wasn't going to happen and her coping skills were failing, Maggie was too proud to listen to her worried significant others. She felt like a failure and was too embarrassed to openly call for help, although she unconsciously gave out verbal and behavioral clues that she was suicidal. "I was hoping someone would step in and help me without my having to openly ask for it." As the situation worsened, Maggie's distorted thinking caused her to withdraw from her mother and friends, and to react defensively when they voiced their concerns.

The most important significant other in Maggie's life was her ex-husband. But since he was the one to break off the relationship, the feelings toward him were volatile, making it difficult for him to try to effectively help her. "It's funny, when my mother and my old roommate from college suggested I see a therapist, I eventually considered it. But when my ex-husband said the same thing, I was enraged. I said, 'Thanks.

Make me look like I've got the problem,'" remembers Maggie. There was only one way in which she could accept his help—if he came back to her.

Maggie was furious with her ex-husband, but would not let herself be openly angry with him. If she could have vented her anger, it could have helped her.

Ironically, it's harder to effectively deal with the anger toward the person with whom we are in conflict. We're afraid of making it worse, often clinging to the hope that the anger will go away and everything will somehow be restored to the remembered idyllic conditions of the past. "I sometimes thought it would have been better if he'd died," says Maggie. The finality of death leaves no room for wasted hope and avoids the pain of being rejected. There's no chance of seeing the other person and reopening old wounds. The person can mourn the loss and move forward with life.

At this point in the suicidal person's thinking process, there are only two alternatives. Either the person's needs can be met by external influences (a rescue, in essence), or the person may try his last option—suicide.

Ambivalence

During the suicidal person's debate between death or a life of pain, another factor enters—ambivalence. Ambivalence, as it applies to suicide, is a simultaneous attraction toward and repulsion from killing oneself. The suicidal person may not want to live, but does not necessarily want to die. He just desperately wants to change the situation he is in. Even if suicide seems to be the only solution, there is still an uncertainty whether to do it. *That uncertainty is your best ally in suicide prevention.*

Dr. Edwin Shneidman described the ambivalence of the typical suicidal state in this way—"A person cuts his or her throat and cries out for help at the same time. Both acts are genuine." There have been people who, after overdosing on pills or slitting their wrists, reconsider and call emergency personnel to save themselves. One teenager, upon changing his mind about suicide, leapt from his speeding car just as it was plummeting over a cliff. He managed to save himself by grabbing a bush growing on the side of the hill. Cut, bruised, and aching, the young man painstakingly pulled himself up the nearly perpendicular, rocky cliff and flagged down a passing car. It's amazing the lengths a suicidal person will sometimes go in order to save his life, even when he's convinced suicide is the only solution.

It is this ambivalence that causes the suicidal person to signal for help and keeps him alive until every shred of hope has been exhausted. Maggie began to signal her despair to friends and co-workers, making more and more comments on how little her life was worth. "When I told my mother I'd be better off dead, I truly believed it, but I really didn't want to kill myself. I was convinced suicide was the only logical solution, but I was hoping—all the time thinking how silly it was—that someone could give me a reason to keep living."

The Suicidal Crisis

Many mental health professionals consider a person to be in a suicidal crisis when he first begins to think about killing himself. Other professionals think of a suicidal crisis as a distinct period of time during which intense despair overrides ambivalence and the person makes a suicide attempt.

This distinct period of time may last only minutes or possibly hours, depending on the person's access to a means of killing himself. If the suicidal person has someone to reach out to and that someone responds, the suicidal person can be kept alive through this period. Then he can again experience ambivalence, and the despair can dissipate.

A small percentage of people are chronically suicidal for several years at a time. These people rely on their suicidal thoughts and behaviors as a coping mechanism, much the same way as an alcoholic uses liquor. Potential rescuers can become confused as to whether the chronically suicidal person is going through a "real" suicidal crisis. They may write off the behavior as being manipulative or "crying wolf." However, chronically suicidal people do commit suicide and should never be dismissed.

Luckily, Maggie's mother kept reaching out to her. "One day, my mother sat me down and asked me point-blank if I wanted to kill myself. She really surprised me, but I couldn't deny it. It was so horrible to admit to my mother, the one who'd given birth to me, that I wanted to die. But it was such a relief. She insisted I see a therapist and said she'd do everything she could for me." For Maggie's mother, it was the most difficult thing she'd ever had to do as a mother, but she says, "Spending one uncomfortable afternoon with my daughter is preferable to losing her and spending the rest of my life kicking myself for not doing something."

Maggie's story is a good illustration of the nature of suicide. First came her emotional distress, her attempts to solve it, the subsequent depression, and distorted thinking. Most important was the ambivalence which caused her to signal her trouble to others. Maggie has recovered and is leading a productive life. Through psychotherapy and a short course of treatment with an antidepressant, she learned new coping skills to help her when further life crises occur, and has resolved her deep feelings toward her own divorce and her parents' divorce. The experience has brought her closer to her mother. "Having gone through this, I think I'm a stronger person," says Maggie. "Every time I experience anything good now, I say, 'See what you might have missed?'"

Four

How Do I Know if the Person Is Serious?

Guidelines for Determining the Person's Danger to Himself

One of the first questions people ask is, "How do I know whether to take the person seriously?" The answer is simple: *Always take any suicidal statement, clue, or gesture seriously.*

The next question—"How can you tell how serious the situation really is?"—is not so easy to answer. Only a mental health professional can determine that.

The following factors are indicators of how serious the situation could be:

A. The person's perception of his own situation—how hopeless he thinks it is and how helpless he feels to change it.

B. Development of the suicide plan—how far along is the person in thinking about or planning the suicide?

C. Most important is the degree of ambivalence—the person's desire to live versus his desire to die.

The following guidelines and examples are simply to give you an idea about the various degrees of risk and a possible response to each.

Before making a final determination of a person's danger to himself, always consult a mental health professional.

Stage 1

Calling for Help

The person is most likely seriously depressed and may be experiencing a high level of anxiety which may interfere with his day-to-day functioning.

His perceptions may be quite distorted. There may be a dramatic difference between the way you see things and the way he sees things, but he may still be able to listen to you.

He probably has no set suicide plan as yet, but is possibly beginning to spend a lot of time thinking about death. He may take foolish risks, flirting with death.

The person could be looking for ways to escape. There is still a high degree of ambivalence and interest in other options, however, thoughts of death may be more frequent.

Your Response: Again, encourage the person to talk. Obtain a promise that he will not hurt himself for a set length of time in order to give you an opportunity to get resources mobilized. Get as many significant others involved as possible and begin the process of getting the person to a mental health professional.

Kelly's Story

Kelly, a cancer survivor, was facing losing her home to foreclosure due to years of medical expenses that had eaten up her savings and salary. She thought about looking for a better paying job, but already in her late fifties, she thought it would be hard to find any job, let alone one that would pay more than her current one. For several months, she grew visibly depressed. Her boss described her performance at work as "listless" and Kelly feared she might get fired.

After a company party at a restaurant, a co-worker, George, was driving behind her. He saw her take some dangerous curves much too fast and a couple of times, she barely avoided careening off the road. George was shocked because Kelly was normally a restrained person and careful driver.

The next day at work, when he admonished her about the incident, she said sadly, "Who cares? It doesn't matter if I live or die anyway."

When George pressed her, Kelly confessed that her finances were a complete mess, she might lose her home, and that she was beginning to consider suicide as a way out of her troubles.

George asked her if she had a plan to kill herself. Kelly said no, she would really rather live, but it just "seemed too difficult."

George was alarmed that her reckless driving was a flirtation with suicide. He knew she was close to her daughter and granddaughter, having seen their photos on Kelly's desk.

"Don't you have a family?" he asked. "Do you really want to hurt them by killing yourself?"

Kelly broke down crying. "But if I lose my home, I'll be a burden on them."

"Losing you would be a much heavier burden," responded George.

Kelly nodded and said he was right, she could never leave her daughter and granddaughter. George got her to promise not to harm herself, and he offered to help her find a mental health professional.

Kelly started seeing a therapist regularly, and with medication and psychotherapy, she began to see things more clearly. She kept her job and was able to refinance her house, although she started looking for a less expensive place to live.

Stage 2

Life at Risk

People in Stage 2 have probably crossed over into a "Life At Risk" position. The individual may be feeling the same as the people in Stage 1, but with greater intensity. He may believe he has no option other than suicide.

The person is probably clinically depressed and may be experiencing high levels of anxiety. His thinking processes may be severely disorganized. He is now pretty convinced that things are hopeless and might have difficulty listening to you.

He may be figuring out possible suicide methods, weighing their pros and cons. His plan is probably beginning to take shape, but is not set. He may give out verbal or behavioral clues that he is suicidal.

There is now an actual desire to die, but he is still ambivalent. No decision to act has been made.

Your Response: Encourage the person to talk. You will probably need to make some decisions and take charge for a brief period of time. Mobilize all possible resources and stay with him, or get others to stay with him, until he is seen by a mental health professional. Do not attempt to deal with this person all by yourself, and do not leave him alone.

Story of Mr. H.

Mr. H., a middle-aged fireman, hurt his back on the job and was in constant pain. While Mr. H. did not require surgery for his injury, his doctor prescribed an opioid to reduce the severity of the pain. Mr. H. grew very depressed over the disability and his doctor's verdict that he could never go back to such physically demanding work without possibly crippling himself completely. He missed the excitement and satisfaction of his job. His other favorite activity was golf, another thing the doctor ordered him to give up.

Mr. H.'s wife tried to get him into less active things like reading and painting while he was recovering from his injury, but he had no interest and spent hours staring blankly at the television. Later, when his back was reasonably healed, Mrs. H. pushed him to get some kind of desk job. The doctor told him his progress was encouraging and, while he would have to take it easy, he could begin taking walks. At this time, the doctor reduced the dosage of opioids with the goal of taking him off the medication entirely.

Mr. H. vehemently disagreed with the doctor because he was still in pain. He said he knew he wasn't any better now and would never get any better in the future. Mr. H. had always been a social drinker, but now with the reduction in his pain medication, his drinking increased as he tried to self-medicate. At this point he just sat around the house drinking, and stopped eating or taking care of his appearance.

He was unable to rouse himself to do anything and ignored invitations from friends. Mrs. H. nagged him about the drinking. She couldn't understand why he couldn't "snap out of it." She saw him as lazy and went off to work each day frustrated and angry. Mr. H. was hurt by her seeming lack of sympathy and they fought constantly.

After a while, Mr. H. developed a morbid preoccupation with methods of dying. It was the only interest he had now, besides drinking. He avidly read stories about suicides and homicides, investigating the efficiency, speed, and imagined amount of pain involved in the deaths. He was vague when his wife asked him why he was interested in such things.

One morning, Mrs. H. pressed until he admitted that all he wanted to do was die. She called Mr. H.'s orthopedist and asked him to recommend a psychotherapist. Mrs. H. took the day off from work and stayed with her husband until he could be seen by the therapist. Eventually, through therapy and the use of antidepressants, Mr. H. learned to adjust to his new physical condition. He decided to stop drinking and started going to Alcoholics Anonymous meetings. Mrs. H. joined him in therapy to work out their marital problems.

Stage 3

Life at High Risk Stage

The person may now feel his life will not get better. He has tried everything he knows and nothing has changed. He's probably feeling hopeless and helpless and may say, "No matter what I do, nothing works."

The person is probably making preparations for death, putting affairs in order, subtly saying goodbyes, writing notes, and planning the best time to accomplish the suicide. He has a definite plan and method to use.

It is likely that he believes death is the only solution, though he is probably still ambivalent—virtually every suicidal person is ambivalent up to the point of the attempt.

Your Response: Get professional help as soon as possible. Call in family members who may be unaware of the seriousness of the situation. If the person has any means of attempting suicide (pills, gun) readily available, remove it immediately. The person may need inpatient psychiatric treatment to save his life.

Mia's Story

Fifteen-year-old Mia had been moody for months. Sometimes she went into rages, screaming, "No one loves me, I might as well just kill myself." Other times she was withdrawn and morose. She had very low self-esteem and felt unloved by everyone. She stopped seeing friends and participating in extracurricular activities at school.

Her mother, June, was concerned, but could see no concrete reason for her daughter to be depressed. June had not realized the degree of constant daily stress that Mia was dealing with, both in the family and at school. Besides, she thought being moody was "part of being a teenager." June believed it would all blow over and Mia would be happy again.

And she was right. Suddenly, Mia seemed to snap out of it. June was relieved to see Mia bouncing around the house, smiling and calm. Mia was getting in touch with friends, and even began texting an old friend who had moved away.

One day, June's son came to her, confused after Mia told him he could have her computer "when she was gone." She had also drilled him on how to take care of her aquarium. June figured Mia was making advance preparations for going away to college in a few years. After all, she'd been doing so well lately, what else could it be?

A couple of days later, one of Mia's teachers called with

disturbing news that June couldn't rationalize away. For some time, the teacher had been noticing Mia's strange mood swings and a drop in the quality of her classwork. A strong obsession with death ran through all of Mia's creative writing assignments. When the teacher disclosed Mia's latest oblique poems about dying, June realize that her daughter must still be depressed.

June sat Mia down and asked her if she'd been feeling suicidal. Mia admitted she had a cache of pills and had been figuring out the best time to kill herself. She'd texted her old friend to say goodbye and was planning goodbye notes to her friends at school, as well as to each member of the family.

When June asked why, Mia broke down and said that she had been questioning her sexuality for some time now, something she felt apprehensive about in their small rural town.

June was shocked, but she faced the facts and took action. First, June forced Mia to hand over the pills. Then, she made an appointment with a local psychiatrist who specialized in working with adolescents. Until Mia could be seen by the psychiatrist, her grandmother came to stay with her while June was at work.

The psychiatrist prescribed a low dosage of an antidepressant and referred Mia to an outpatient psychotherapist who also specialized in working with adolescents. The psychotherapist recommended that the whole family go into therapy to work on family relationships and interactions. With this combination of medication, outpatient therapy, and the wholehearted support of her family, teacher, and several friends, hospitalization was not necessary.

Stage 4

Suicide Attempt

When the person does something to himself that could bring about his death—for example, taking an overdose of pills or cutting his wrist—that is a Suicide Attempt. Taking only a couple of pills or merely scratching his wrist is a Suicide Gesture. On the other hand, a Suicide Gesture qualifies as a Suicide Attempt if the person thought that it would result in death. Even if it couldn't possibly result in the person's death, do not dismiss a Suicide Gesture. The person must be in great distress to go to such lengths. Also, many people have died accidentally as a result of Suicide Gestures.

Your Response: First, treat this situation as a medical emergency.

1. If the person is unconscious or losing consciousness, dial 9-1-1. The dispatcher may ask you questions about the situation. Tell him that this is a suicide attempt. Describe the method used, when the attempt took place, and the attempter's present condition. Ask the dispatcher what you can do for the suicide attempter until the emergency services arrive.

2. If the person is conscious and refuses treatment, call the emergency room of the nearest hospital or your family doctor. Explain what is happening and ask for advice.

If the doctor says the suicide attempter should be seen for treatment, but the attempter still refuses to go voluntarily, call your local mental health center, suicide crisis line, or a mental health professional. Describe the situation and ask for instructions on how to go about getting treatment for a person on an involuntary basis. Let them guide you through the subsequent steps, for a "petition for evaluation and involuntary treatment." Rules and procedures vary from state to state.

In almost all states, a suicide attempt is more than enough grounds for a "petition for evaluation and involuntary treatment." Also, you don't need to be a relative of the suicidal person to get the petition.

This petition is not committing the person to long-term treatment, but allows emergency personnel or law enforcement officers to take him to the emergency room for evaluation by a physician. In most states, a magistrate or probate judge can sign an order for emergency evaluation by a physician. In a given number of working days (three to five in most states) the suicidal person is re-evalutated by a physician to determine if he should be committed for longer term treatment or referred for outpatient treatment.

Note: You may not have to complete the entire involuntary commitment process. Many suicidal people realize their need for treatment and agree to be hospitalized voluntarily.

Remove any implements the person could use to kill himself, i.e., guns, knives or other sharp objects, ropes, pills, poisons, etc. Don't just hide them from the suicidal person—remove them completely from his home.

Do not leave the suicide attempter alone. Involve as many mental health professionals, family members, friends, etc., as possible.

Do not allow the suicide attempter to talk you out of taking action.

In drug overdoses or self-poisonings, call 9-1-1 immediately. If the person is conscious, ask what he took, how many pills, or how much of the poison he has taken. Also ask whether alcohol was used in addition to the pills or other substances. If the attempter is unconscious, find the pill bottle or poison container and try to determine how much was taken. Whether the person is conscious or unconscious, bring the pill bottle or poison container, and any sample of the substances left over, to the emergency room. This could help in treating the patient.

Above all, do not give the suicide attempter a choice in whether or not he receives treatment. The only choice is whether he goes voluntarily or involuntarily.

Alan's Story

After his mother's death, Kevin was prepared for his father's grief and depression, but he became alarmed when his father, Alan, didn't seem to pull out of it or adjust to the loss. Alan only went out of the house for groceries, and even stopped going to church. He was losing weight and seemed very withdrawn. Kevin was aware that his father was in a high risk group for suicide because of his age and the significance of his loss. Shortly before the first anniversary of his mother's death, Kevin gathered the courage to talk to his father about suicide.

Alan tried to brush off his son's observations, but Kevin didn't give up. He asked Alan gently, but firmly, "Are you so lonesome for Mom that you've thought about killing yourself?"

Alan acted offended by the question. Then Kevin asked him the most important question: "How do you plan to kill yourself?" Alan responded with a well thought-out plan that included updating his will, paying off several outstanding bills, and collecting enough pills to "do the job." After listening to his father talk about his feelings for several hours, Kevin forced him to hand over the pills and told him that he was not going to leave him alone for one minute until he was assured Alan would not commit suicide.

Alan and Kevin fell asleep talking. Later that night, Kevin was awakened by a gunshot. He ran to his father's room and found him lying semiconscious, his skull grazed by a bullet. Kevin had said and done all the right things, but hadn't realized that often, the suicidal person has backup methods to kill himself. He called 9-1-1, but Alan mumbled, "Just let me die. I just want to die." At the hospital, Kevin called the family priest to stay with Alan while he petitioned for involuntary treatment.

Alan, a Vietnam veteran, was transferred to the nearest VA hospital, where he recovered from his wounds and began psychotherapy and taking antidepressants. Kevin kept closely involved in his father's treatment and continued to watch for suicidal behavior. The psychotherapist made Kevin aware that once the barrier between suicidal thought and action is crossed, subsequent suicide attempts are easier to make if the conditions haven't improved.

Alan's story has a happy ending. Alan continued antidepressants and outpatient therapy at the VA after he was released from the hospital. With plenty of support from family and friends, Alan began to work through his grief and climb out of his depression. While he could never replace his wife, he found new interests that gave him reasons to keep living.

Get Help

The 988 Suicide and Crisis Lifeline
Call or text 988.
www.988lifeline.org
Formerly known as the National Suicide Prevention Lifeline. (The 1-800-273-8255 phone number still works.)

This is a national network of local crisis centers that provide free confidential and emotional support to people in a suicidal crisis or emotional distress. They operate 24/7.

Crisis Text Line
Text "HOME" to 741741

Substance Abuse and Mental Health Services Administration (SAMHSA)
1-800-662-HELP (4357)
Service is available 24/7 in English and Spanish.
www.samhsa.gov

Alcohol & Drug Help Line
1-800-923-4357

YouthLine
1-877-968-8491
Text "teen2teen" to 839863
www.theyouthline.org

Help for Veterans:

According to the CDC, suicide rates are higher among veterans than non-veterans, and suicide is the second leading cause of death among veterans under age 45.

Veterans Crisis Line/Military Crisis Line
Dial 988 and Press 1
Text 838255
www.veteranscrisisline.net

Help for LGBTQ Youth:

Young people who identify as LGBTQ have a higher rate of suicide attempts than heterosexual youths, according to the CDC.

The Trevor Project

Crisis intervention and suicide prevention for LGBTQ youth. Call 1-866-488-7386 or Text "TREVOR" to 678678. Or connect via online chat at *www.thetrevorproject.org.*

In addition, most communities have suicide prevention centers, mental health centers, or mental health clinics. Some cities have suicide prevention centers that offer various services around the clock. They offer information, counseling, and therapy, and some operate 24-hour emergency services. Online, search for "suicide prevention" or listings of hospitals, religious organizations, and psychiatric referral services under "mental health services" or look in a phone directory under "mental health information" and "treatment centers and counselors." Other sources for information are local universities with medical schools, your family doctor or clergyman, and the emergency room of your local hospital.

Information In Non-Emergencies

For more information, including a listing of community mental health centers throughout the country contact:

The National Institute of Mental Health
6001 Executive Boulevard, MSC 9663
Bethesda, MD 20892-9663
Tel. 1-866-615-6464 (toll-free)
Email them at *nimhinfo@nih.gov*.

You can call the American Association of Suicidology during business hours at 1-888-9PREVENT, or write them at 448 Walton Avenue, # 790, Hummelstown, PA. 17036; *www.suicidology.org*.
Email for general inquiries: *info@suicidology.org*
This is not a crisis center, but can refer you to crisis centers in your area and send you information on suicide prevention.

If you are having difficulty locating a mental health center, go to Mental Health America's website: *www.mhanational.org*.
Again, these are referral organizations, not emergency centers, and are open during regular business hours.

Never hesitate to call a mental health professional if you suspect that someone is suicidal. Always seek professional guidance in handling these situations.

Five

How Do I Talk to the Suicidal Person?

Opening Up Communication

A suicidal person's isolation is probably the biggest risk factor in suicide. Breaking that isolation is the key to suicide prevention. How do you approach someone who is signaling his distress, but has not directly asked for intervention? How do you reach out to the suicidal person?

As stated earlier, suicidal behavior can be seen as a form of communication, a last desperate cry for help. But there can be a mismatch in communication that may result in you and the suicidal person being at cross purposes. The suicidal person may put on a happy facade and try to convince you that nothing's wrong—even to the point of denying that an unsuccessful suicide attempt was indeed a suicide attempt. He can make you doubt yourself and feel like you've read too much into his situation. Or, the suicidal person can be off-putting and difficult to handle.

Added to your own discomfort with the situation, this can make you shy away. You may become frustrated, stressed, and anxious when trying to deal with the person's negative attitude and illogical arguments regarding his problems.

You may also be tempted to give the troubled person a lot of space in an attempt to be helpful. Don't assume, "He'll talk when he's ready to talk." Leaving him alone adds to the sense of isolation he may be experiencing. You may have to force yourself to make the first move.

Most important, don't be afraid that asking about suicidal intentions will "give the person ideas." Just remember, the decision to commit suicide comes from within the person—you cannot make him decide to kill himself.

You may also fear that if you're wrong and the person you're concerned about is not suicidal, your questions will make him angry with you. Trust your instincts if you suspect someone is suicidal. Keep in mind that it's better to risk annoying a friend or family member than to risk losing him forever to suicide.

Your reaching out and being there for the person is the most important thing. You do not have to say all the right words to help the suicidal person. Demonstrating your interest and caring will mean more to him than anything else. The best way to do that is by listening to him.

This chapter is not designed to teach you how to counsel the suicidal person. You will learn how to open up communication so that he feels less alone, which will aid you in getting him help from a mental health professional.

You may feel that your relationship with the suicidal person is too conflicted, or you may not have the confidence to talk to him. Don't feel bad about it—talking about suicide is a difficult thing to do. However, if you see suicidal signs in a person and don't feel you can talk to him, find another significant other who can. You can also get a mental health professional involved. Most communities have local mental health centers or suicide hotlines for advice or referral. The important thing is that, somehow, the suicidal person gets help.

*What **Not** to Say to a Suicidal Person*

Seventy-five-year-old Harry remembers a conversation with his daughter prior to his suicide attempt. "When I told my daughter I wanted to kill myself, she became unglued. She said, 'How can you even say such a thing, Dad? These are your golden years, the best years of your life.' I said, 'If these are my best years, then I want to die now.' And she laughed kind of nervously and said, 'You don't really mean that, Dad, do you?' I said, 'No,' because I knew that's what she wanted to hear. I realized then that I couldn't talk to her about it. It was like we were speaking different languages."

When someone expresses suicidal feelings, you must stop yourself from automatically responding with misinformed clichés. Though the intentions may be good, the effects can cut off communication and actually make the suicidal person feel worse. Here are some things you should avoid saying:

"Don't say things like that!"—This immediately shuts the door on communication.

"You haven't been considering suicide, have you?"—Phrasing the question negatively implies you want to hear the answer "no."

"It's all in your mind. Things aren't that bad."—This discounts his problems (although it may be helpful to remind him of the good things in his life).

"You'll feel better after you've had a good night's rest (or dinner, or gotten over him/her, or gone shopping, etc.)"—It's likely that he's already found that his usual coping methods have failed and he must find better solutions.

"You'll snap out of it if you really want to."—This could make him feel even more helpless and guilty about how bad he feels.

"You're only hurting yourself."—To the suicidal person, this may sound like it doesn't matter to you whether he kills himself or not. Let him know suicide affects everyone in contact with the person, especially family.

"You don't really mean it. You're only saying this to get attention."—He wouldn't say it if he didn't mean it. He *is* trying to get your attention in order to save his life.

These are some specific things you shouldn't say to teenagers:

"I made it through my teen years, you've only got a couple more left."—This trivializes the problems of being a teenager, making him think that if he can't handle his problems now, there's no hope of handling adult problems.

"You've got your whole life ahead of you."—That's exactly what the suicidal young person perceives as the problem.

"These are the best years of your life."—If the young person has problems now, he may decide he doesn't want to stick around to see the rest of his life.

What to Say

You may wonder, "What should I say?" One thing to keep in mind is to use "I" statements whenever possible (begin your sentences with "I" instead of "You"). This is less threatening and less likely to make the suicidal person feel defensive. It may also be helpful to use the person's name when opening the conversation and wherever else it seems natural. Using the person's name is more personal and may help him regain his sense of identity, may aid in assisting him in concentrating on his issues, and lets him know that you are focused on him.

The following are some common statements made by suicidal people and possible helpful responses to each:

> **Suicidal Person:** "I have nothing to live for."
> **Your Response:** "That's not how I see it, Kyle. Tell me more about how you see things."

The most important thing is to get the suicidal person talking about how he feels and to simply listen to him. Having a chance to air out his problems could provide him some temporary relief. Feeling like he has a friend to confide in may help lift his low self-image.

You may want to cite the positive things in the person's life—his accomplishments, talents, personality strengths, or activities he enjoys—as long as you're not arguing with the suicidal person. Don't say, "But you're wrong. You have this, this, and this to live for." Try to point out things he may not be seeing at the time. If hard pressed, mention activities he has enjoyed in the past.

If he starts arguing, back off. For example, if you point out that the suicidal person has a wonderful, loving family and he says, "But they don't care about me," don't dispute it.

Just get him talking about his problems again.

You could tell him there are solutions to problems and give some him suggestions. Remind him that dying is not a valid choice and is irrevocable. You could suggest, "Let's try this instead." Tell him help is available for his problems.

> **Suicidal Person:** "The situation is hopeless."
> **Your Response:** "I know how hard it is for you to imagine the situation will ever get better, but it can. I know that when I've struggled with problems for a long time, I've gotten really confused and felt that it was hopeless. I went to a therapist and she was able to help me sort things out."

An elderly, chronically ill, or terminally ill person might talk about being a burden to you if you are taking care of him. You could stress to him that just having him around is worth it. His suicide, however, would be overwhelming.

> **Suicidal Person:** "I don't want to be a burden on you. I won't be if I kill myself."
> **Your Response:** "You're not a burden on me. The real burden would be if you killed yourself."

The most important thing you can say is, "You matter to me. I care about you," and really mean it. Your act of reaching out to the suicidal person can reinforce that.

> **Suicidal Person:** "You'll be better off without me."
> **Your Response:** "No, I won't. I'd be devastated if you killed yourself, Mom."
> **Suicidal Person:** "No one cares about me."
> **Your Response:** "I care about you. I'm very concerned about you."

Avoid existential arguments about the morality of suicide. Don't argue with the person over whether or not he has the right to kill himself. He may be caught in a web of circular thinking and probably has difficulty thinking rationally. Debating about life vs. death and the merits of suicide could backfire.

> **Suicidal Person:** "We all die eventually, what does it matter if I take care of it now?"
> **Your Response:** "It matters to me. I care about you. I don't want to miss all of the things we might do together."

Families and friends tend to have more problems dealing with a loved one's death by suicide (increased guilt, anger, and the stigma of suicide) than families and friends who are dealing with a natural death.

> **Suicidal Person:** "It's my life to do with as I wish."
> **Your Response:** "It isn't only your life. If you kill yourself, it will have an affect on everyone around you."

Suicidal adults (particularly mothers) with children are often less likely to kill themselves. They may become depressed, desperate, and suicidal, but they tend to hang on for their children. Point out to the suicidal person the damage that killing himself would inflict on his children—the immediate consequences of losing a parent at an early age, the stigma of suicide, as well as the risk of psychological problems farther down the line.

If you're talking to a teenager, you could cite teenage suicide clusters. Tell him that his suicide could influence his peers at school, and if given media coverage (either mainstream media or social media), possibly a teenager in some other city.

Things to Remember

Be direct. If someone gives you a verbal clue, don't shy away from the issue. Ask straightforwardly, "Are you considering suicide?" or "Are you thinking of killing yourself?"

If the troubled person exhibits suicidal behavior clues, such as writing a will, buying a gun, etc., it is a good idea to inquire specifically about it—"I've been noticing that you seem pretty down lately and that you've recently bought a gun (or written a will). Are you planning to kill yourself?" If the answer is yes, a good response to open up a discussion may be, "Let's talk about your suicidal feelings."

Be calm. The suicidal person can get overwrought when bringing up such deep emotions, and your remaining calm will help him settle down. It is also possible that the person will seem outwardly calm, but is actually experiencing tremendous turmoil and confusion inside. If he shows little or no emotion, do not mistake that for inner peace or control.

You should not blame others in the family or circle of friends for the person's feelings. If the suicidal person blames someone else for his wanting to die and is doing it to "make him sorry," you could say, "Another person is not worth killing yourself over." By that same token, you should not blame yourself. The suicidal person's feelings of worthlessness usually are the result of a combination of long-term influences.

Even after a successful talk with the suicidal person, don't be lulled into thinking that everything's going to be all right now, even if the suicidal person seems to have recovered completely. Serious depression does not lift overnight. The troubled person may feel an initial, but temporary, sense of relief after finally unlocking his secret.

Another reason for a sudden, apparent recovery may be that he's made the decision to go ahead and commit suicide. Many people in this position experience a sense of calm, even elation, now that their minds are made up. This is an extremely dangerous situation. The lifting of depression gives them the energy to carry out their plans and misleads the significant others into relaxing their vigilance.

Don't let the suicidal person convince you, or himself, that the crisis is over until he has seen a mental health professional. Many follow-up suicide attempts occur within the first couple of weeks after an initial attempt. Don't let your guard down. You must also remain alert for suicidal behavior even after the person has been seen by a therapist.

Don't feel bad if you must employ manipulation in a dire suicidal emergency. If the suicidal person has a gun to his head or is ready to leap off a ledge, tell him whatever he needs to hear to make him change his mind.

Try not to get angry or frustrated. If you have trouble getting the person to open up, don't give up. Keep trying.

Sample Dialogue—Tom's Case

The following is a hypothetical dialogue to illustrate the fine points of reaching out to the suicidal person. It is meant only as a guideline. No conversation will go exactly like this. Depending on the conversation, the order of the steps may be changed. That's all right, as long as you hit the major items at some point.

Step 1—Gather Your Courage and Talk to the Person

Try to find a private and neutral location. If that's not possible, ask if you can come over to the person's house, or invite him to come to yours. It is best to talk with the person face to face, but if you can't, talk with him over the phone. Any contact is better than none.

Approach the person you are worried about in a positive and supportive manner. Have your opening statements well thought out. Do not simply ask, "Is everything okay?" or "How is everything?" It makes it too easy for the person to give a simple "Yes" or "Everything's fine." Do not ask leading questions such as, "Is your marriage the problem?" Remember, you're not a counselor. Express your concern for the person and give him specific examples of why you are concerned.

Remember to address the person by name and use "I" statements. Statements that begin with "you" are likely to put the person on the defensive. Open with "I am concerned about you," or "I get the feeling you're troubled. Is something bothering you?"

> **You:** Tom, I've been meaning to talk to you for some time now. I've really missed you since you dropped out of the bowling league. What's going on?
> **Tom:** Oh, it's nothing. I just don't feel well. Must be a virus.
> **You:** What does your doctor say about it?
> **Tom:** I haven't seen him. It's no big deal, it'll pass.

Be prepared for initial evasiveness. Don't ignore your gut

feeling about the suicidal clues you've been receiving from the person. If you feel he is in danger, talk to him about it. It is sometimes difficult to actually come out and ask him. Often it's even more difficult for him to admit that he's got a problem. Always remember that the suicidal person doesn't necessarily want to die, he just wants to get out of the situation he is in. He needs your persistence, and he wants your help—even if he acts otherwise.

> **You:** Tom, a virus doesn't last for months. I'm going to be honest with you. I see you withdrawing from everybody, and I am concerned. Please tell me what's bothering you.
> **Tom:** Nobody wants to listen to another person's problems. Everybody's got their own.
> **You:** I'm your friend, and what are friends for?

If the person is angry or hostile, don't be put off. Don't take his anger and hostility personally. He may be angry at his spouse, his employer, himself, or the whole world. Be persistent.

> **You:** Tom, I need to talk to you.
> **Tom:** Well, I don't want to talk to you. Why is everybody on my back lately?
> **You:** Do you have a few minutes?
> **Tom:** No, I'm busy.

You can't force someone to talk to you. If he continues to put you off, you can agreeably press for another meeting, and alert others to your concerns about the situation. **But if you think the person may be in immediate danger, call for help right away and don't leave him alone.** Most community mental health centers have after-hours emergency services. If you know a therapist, call and ask for an emergency appointment. If you don't know a therapist, call your family doctor, clergyman, local hospital, or medical school for a referral. It may become necessary to hospitalize the person in a psychiatric treatment facility.

> **You:** Let's talk tomorrow. Could we get together for lunch?
> **Tom:** I'm really not in the mood.

Don't give up. Try to get him to talk about something less threatening.

> **You:** Are you having trouble sleeping? You seem a little frazzled.
> **Tom:** Well, yeah. I've only been getting a couple hours a night if I'm lucky.
> **You:** Is something wrong?
> **Tom:** Maybe. But you don't really want to hear about it.

Don't argue with the suicidal person about anything other than whether or not you care about him. Often you are being tested. The suicidal person needs reassurance. You may need to state emphatically that you care. Show him how you feel by your persistence.

> **You:** Yes, I do. I care about you very much, Tom.
> **Tom:** It doesn't concern you, so quit badgering me and mind your own business.
> **You:** It's hard to mind my own business when a good friend appears to be so troubled.
> **Tom:** Okay, it's my marriage. But there isn't anything anybody can do. The whole thing seems pretty hopeless.
> **You:** I may not be able to do much except listen, but I'm willing to do that. (Or you may simply repeat what the person has said in the form of a question: "What do you mean by hopeless?")

Step 2—Listen, Listen, Listen

Now be quiet and listen very carefully to what the person says. Giving him your full attention will help boost his sagging self-esteem. Be supportive and don't judge. *You do not have to make comments or have all the answers.* A nod or a "Uh-huh" is sufficient. The most important thing you can do for the suicidal person is listen to him. Listen not only to what's being said, but also to the way in which it is being said.

Be patient if the person is hesitant as he speaks. He may be unaccustomed to delving into, let alone sharing, deep emotions. He might be censoring himself, sounding out in his head what he's going to say to you. Allow him to open up. Don't jump in to avoid awkward silences and keep the conversation going. The usual rules of polite conversation do not apply here.

> **Tom:** I'm so confused. I thought things were going great, but about three months ago, Cathy came out and said she's so unhappy she doesn't know if she wants to stay in the marriage. I didn't even see this coming. What's wrong with me?

Use reflective statements or questions. It's okay to phrase them with "you" because it's simply reflecting back what the person said.

> **You:** What makes you think there's something wrong with you?
>
> **Tom:** Well, it just immobilized me. It was days before I could function. I just sat around the house. It was like my world had come to an end. I'm just so confused by this whole thing. I know I must seem pretty childish, unable to handle my own problems.

Step 3—Be Supportive

The suicidal person may think he's hit rock bottom in having asked for help and may be worried about appearing weak and needy. Buoy the person's self-confidence.

> **You:** Asking for help is a sign of strength. Admitting you have a problem is a difficult, courageous thing to do. I'm glad you feel you can talk to me.
>
> **Tom:** You don't think I'm crazy?

Many suicidal people are frightened and ashamed of feeling the way they do. They wonder if being suicidal means they are "crazy." Try to normalize the person's feelings by letting him know that others would feel the same way in similar circumstances.

> **You:** No, I'm sure if I were in your shoes, I'd feel the same way. Most people would if their whole lives just turned upside down.

If he's still anxious about the way he feels, you might add:

> **You:** Emotional ups and downs are natural. We wouldn't have full lives without them. Everyone feels this way from time to time. We wouldn't be thinking, feeling people if we didn't.

If the person says he's depressed and feels bad about being depressed, you could tell him:

> **You:** Hey, everyone gets depressed, especially when something like this happens. It's natural.

Stress that depression is temporary and treatable, while suicide is permanent.

> **You:** I know you may not believe me right now, but you won't feel this way all the time. Depression is treatable. Death is not.

If you've gone through a similar experience, it might be helpful to mention it, but avoid the temptation to talk about yourself. Keep the focus on the distressed person.

Use "how," "what," "when," or "where" while asking questions about feelings. Do not use "why." "Why" questions are often unanswerable, dead-end questions. It can be difficult for people to articulate *why* they feel a certain way, and they often find it's much easier to talk about *how* they feel. You could say, "How did you get to this point?" instead of "Why did you get to this point?"

You: How are you feeling about things now?
Tom: Hurt! I feel really hurt. And angry. Why didn't she say something sooner? She gives me this whole laundry list of complaints, then walks out. At first I was so angry I wanted to hurt her. But I can't do that, so I want to hurt myself.

Don't appear shocked by what the suicidal person says. Don't try to lighten up the situation by making jokes, or attempt to change how the person feels. Accept how he is feeling, even if it makes you feel uncomfortable.

Step 4—Ask Him if He's Suicidal

You: When you say, "I want to hurt myself," do you mean you want to kill yourself?
Tom: Yeah, I've given a lot of thought to offing myself.

Be very direct. Use words such as "suicide," "death," "dying," "kill," etc. Don't use euphemisms such as "offing yourself." Death is death. Do not be overly subtle with it.

You: I don't understand. Does "offing myself" mean you're thinking about killing yourself?
Tom: Yeah. It's the only way out.
You: Out of what?
Tom: Out of the mess I'm in.
You: You feel the only way out is death?
Tom: Well, I can't go on this way. If there was any other way out, I wouldn't be talking about suicide, would I?

Suicidal people often get into circular thinking. They are unable to see options and choices, and the conversation can continue around and around. This can be frustrating, but try not to let it get to you.

Step 5—Offer Other Options

Once the person has opened up about his problem—and you're sure he feels that you've listened to him—try to offer him at least one concrete suggestion of how to deal with it. But don't set yourself up as his counselor.

> **You:** Have you talked to a marriage counselor? My sister and her husband were so close to a divorce, they had even hired lawyers. They talked to a counselor before it went any further and he really helped a lot. I can get his name from my sister.

You have just offered Tom a possible way to deal with his problems and some hope for saving his marriage. You have also normalized the whole situation by talking about people who have been in his place and have been helped.

> **Tom:** Cathy mentioned going to see a counselor a while ago, but I was so mad I didn't even want to talk about it. What if she won't go now?
> **You:** It might be a good idea to see someone on your own to help you get through these hard times.

Or you could say—

> **You:** If I were you, I'd see a therapist just to help me get through these hard times.

If the person balks about seeking therapy, tell him that his being suicidal means he needs professional help that you as a friend can't give him. If he's very reluctant, offer to contact the therapist yourself, and even offer to go with the person to the first appointment.

It is also helpful to determine how the person coped with major problems in the past. Use your knowledge of the person's history. If he's made previous suicide attempts or felt suicidal in the past, be extra alert.

Step Six—Discuss the Suicide Plan

Even if the person has agreed to see a therapist, you should try to find out about his suicide plan.

You: Do you have a plan to kill yourself?
Tom: Well, I've got this gun. I bought it for protection from burglars.
You: When are you planning to do it?
Tom: I don't know. I don't have a time planned out. It's just here when I need it.

Ask specific details about the suicide plan. Ask for details about the suicide plan. If the person has a definite plan and the means to carry it out, you should stay with him until he can see a mental health professional. Make sure he doesn't have multiple plans. Remove guns, knives, pills, or any other means which the person could use to kill himself.

You: Do you have any alternate plans?
Tom: No, just the gun.
You: I want you to give me the gun. We'll go to your house right now.
Tom: Okay. Please don't tell anyone about this...

Don't let the person swear you to secrecy regarding his suicidal intentions. You can promise to keep the other information confidential, but tell him you might have to relay his danger to a network of others.

You: I'm very concerned about these feelings. I promise not to talk about the problems with your marriage, but I can't keep your suicidal plans a secret.

Step Seven—Get the Person to Professional Help

Call the therapist yourself if the suicidal person can't, and offer to go to the first session with him. Get the person to promise not to do anything to harm himself until he can see a professional. Don't ask for a commitment longer than twenty-four hours, or until he sees the therapist. Staying with the suicidal person is the safe thing to do during that twenty-four hour period prior to seeing the mental health professional.

You: I've made an appointment for you to see the therapist

> tomorrow at 3:00. Will you promise me that you won't hurt yourself between now and then?
>
> **Tom:** Okay, I promise. But can I call you if it gets really rough?
>
> **You:** Of course. I'm here for you anytime.

It's a good idea to help him structure his time until his appointment with the therapist. The suicidal person may have lost control over his life and may need you to take charge.

> **You:** How will you get by until you see the therapist? Let's go to a movie tonight. Maybe get some dinner after?

Or:

> **You:** How about I get us something to eat and we watch the game on TV?

Offer to help in any way you can and stay in touch with the suicidal person while he is in the process of getting together with the therapist. Help him figure out ways to keep occupied until the appointment. Encourage him to call a suicide hotline or prevention center if he feels suicidal. Make sure he has the phone numbers handy. Follow through and verify that the person is getting the help of a mental health professional. However, *if you think that the person is in immediate danger, stay with him or call in someone else to stay with him—do not leave the person alone.*

Talking to someone about his suicidal feelings isn't easy. To effectively deal with the suicidal person, you should first deal with your own fears about suicide. The suicidal person may remind you of your own problems and your own depression or thoughts of suicide. Don't let yourself be threatened by the suicidal person's thoughts of killing himself. Don't take his suicidal urge personally. He may be caught in tunnel vision and may not even be thinking about you at this time. Don't take his suicidal wish as a judgment call on your own life, or as a finger pointing at supposed inadequacies in your relationship with him. Dwelling on your relationship is a waste of time and energy at this point. It is a matter of life and death to get the suicidal person to professional help.

If you are feeling pressured and overwhelmed, the most important things to remember are:

1. You are not to attempt to counsel the person. Your role is to reach out and guide him to the professional help he needs.

2. Don't try to go it alone. Call on other friends, relatives, etc., to help you deal with the situation.

3. While your positive actions may save someone, you are not responsible for his life.

4. If you don't feel you are able to talk to the suicidal person, find another significant other or mental health professional who can.

5. Dealing with a suicidal loved one can be very stressful. Professional psychotherapy may be helpful if you start to feel overwhelmed and depressed about the situation. It can be difficult to help the suicidal person if you're having emotional problems yourself.

Don't be surprised if you fail to get the person to open up. Even experienced therapists fail with certain patients. If your efforts are rebuffed, put aside any feelings of anger or rejection and give it another shot. Get others involved and keep trying.

Keep your perspective when dealing with the suicidal person. Don't let him persuade you that his life truly is hopeless and that he has a legitimate reason to be suicidal. Remember that there are many people in the same or worse circumstances who are not suicidal—whether they're terminally ill, severely disabled, mourning extensive losses, destitute, or persecuted politically—who manage to find a reason to live.

Whenever you may be tempted to justify another's suicidal feelings, always remember that even in the darkest moments, there is room for hope. Don't buy into the suicidal person's point of view. Things can turn around, but only if the person is still alive.

Stress to the suicidal person that even during the worst of times, it's better to live and solve his problems, and that you care enough to make sure he does.

Special Cases—Talking to Elderly or Young People

For the most part, the instructions for talking with suicidal people of all ages is basically the same, though there are special considerations for the elderly and the young.

Suggestions for Dealing with the Elderly

Seniors are less likely than younger people to give out clues that they are suicidal, and their suicide attempts tend to be more lethal. The elderly are generally more isolated since they are more likely to be retired, widowed or divorced, or have outlived friends and family. They may feel out of step with today's world and ignored by the public and the media. Failing health is often cited as a major cause of suicide among the elderly, but it's also likely feelings of isolation, uselessness, and worthlessness that create the depression and suicidal feelings.

Loss of self-sufficiency is a major contributing factor. Some older people choose suicide over dependency on others or being institutionalized in a nursing home. If your elderly parent says he wants to kill himself because he's a burden to you, you could tell him what he means to you and how much you value having him around. You might say, "I love you very much. I still learn a lot from you and value our relationship." You might ask for information about your family, or what life was like in the past, in order to help him feel like he's contributing. If no one could bake bread like your mother, encourage her to do so if it makes her feel happy and useful. You can give away the excess.

If there was an activity or special talent the elderly person enjoyed once, but quit because of the time demands of working and raising a family, encourage him to take it up again. For example, Harry, the elderly man mentioned earlier, painted as a young man and dreamed of becoming an artist. He put aside this ambition when his father died and he had to get a job to support the family. Eventually, Harry got married and had a family of his own to support.

When he retired after a lifetime of supporting loved ones, he felt useless. His wife died, sending Harry into depression. Depression grew into despair, and Harry began to talk of killing himself. Alerted, his children sought the help of a psychiatrist who prescribed antidepressants and referred Harry to a local psychologist for individual psychotherapy.

After several sessions, the therapist recommended Harry take up painting again. Happily, he is no longer suicidal. His therapist cites Harry's return to his early love of painting—more than psychotherapy—for this turnaround. Harry says another late-blooming painter, Grandma Moses, is his inspiration.

If taking care of an older relative is difficult, it's okay for you to be honest. You could say:

> "Sometimes our relationship is strained and yes, taking care of you is often tough, but I'm willing to do that. You took care of me at one time. What I've gained from you over the years more than offsets the burden."

The most important thing you can do for the suicidal elderly person is to be in closer contact and show interest in his care. Ask how he's feeling physically and emotionally, and whether you can do anything to help. Include the elderly person in your activities. Ask his advice in important matters—the elderly person's experience counts for a lot.

Dealing with a Suicidal Youth

Some adults find it difficult to take a child's or teenager's suicidal intentions seriously. They think of their children as being too young to have serious problems and discount their suicidal feelings.

Although suicide can occur in any family, many parents feel like failures if their child is suicidal, therefore, they deny it. Parents may not want to believe that their children could ever really be suicidal. But young people are as capable of feeling despair as adults and, judging from their high suicide rate, they are capable of taking their lives.

Sometimes young children will speak about wanting to die or wanting to kill themselves, but more often children who are experiencing suicidal thoughts may not express them in words. Instead, look for clues in their behavior. A child might become preoccupied with death or suicide. You might see this in the shows they watch on TV, websites they visit, what they write in journals, or in games they play.

>   **You:** I've noticed that everything you're watching on TV is about death. I'm concerned. Are you thinking about death a lot of the time?
>   **Child:** I just like that stuff. I wish I were dead sometimes.
>   **You:** Why?
>   **Child:** I feel like I'm different from the other kids. If I weren't here, I wouldn't feel so bad all the time.
>   **You:** I am sorry you feel so bad. Let's talk about this.

It often takes a bit more persistence to get adolescents to open up than adults. Adolescents can be extremely self-conscious and often dread being considered a "loser." They can act angry and hostile if they are masking their depression, or they can be withdrawn and closed up. Either way, it's a good idea to give them a broad opening:

>   **You:** It looks to me like you need to talk things over with someone.
>   **Youth:** No, I don't. It doesn't matter anyway.
>   **You:** I'm really concerned about you. What do you mean it doesn't matter?
>   **Youth:** Leave me alone. I don't want to talk with you.

If you're a parent, you may find that sometimes it's difficult for your child to talk about his problems with you. Your child may feel that he's letting you down or fear your rejection. A child's worst fear is that his parents don't love him. He may feel that he can't discuss the problem with you especially if it involves something you might disapprove of, like drugs, sex, or crime.

If your child doesn't want to talk to you, ask who he would like to talk with—an older sibling, another relative, a peer, a teacher, or a therapist. Don't feel like a failure as a parent. Making sure he talks to someone—anyone he trusts—is the best thing you can do.

If you're a non-parent significant other in the young person's life (whether another relative, teacher, or peer), the suicidal young person may try to make you swear not to tell his parents. Never make such a promise. It can be especially difficult if you're a peer of the suicidal youth, but it's better to have a friend alive and angry with you than dead. Tell him you must speak to others—especially his family—about his suicidal intentions. However, it's all right to promise that you won't divulge details about *why* he's suicidal.

When broaching the subject of suicide with an adolescent, you may need to start subtly.

> **You:** I've noticed you seem troubled lately. Sometimes when a person's problems get to be too much for him, he may just feel like going to sleep and never waking up. Have you ever felt like that?
> **Youth:** Yeah.
> **You:** Have you been thinking about killing yourself?
> **Youth:** Yeah, sometimes it seems like that would solve everything.

Try to talk with the young person, not *at* him. Once he is talking, never patronize him or discount his feelings. Treat him like an adult.

> **You:** What problems would it solve?
> **Youth:** My whole life. I'm better off dead. You're better off without me.
> **You:** But I don't think I'd be better off without you. I'd be devastated if I lost you.

He may feel the need to test you.

> **Youth:** You don't care. You don't love me. Nobody loves me.

You: I love you very much. I've been so busy lately, maybe I haven't let you know how much I love you and how much I care about you. I want to help you.
Youth: You can't. It's hopeless.
You: What's hopeless?
Youth: Oh, just everything. I flunked my history test today. I didn't make the track team, either. And nobody asked me to the prom. I'm just too ugly, I guess. All my friends have been asked and I know they're saying things behind my back.

In the broad scope of things, you might find the problems of a teenager minor compared to adult problems. But to the young person, these things are important. Years ago, the media ran a story about a teenager who killed herself after being caught smoking cigarettes. She stated in a suicide note that she was afraid she'd be put on restriction for a year. Many young people haven't had enough life experiences to know that the downs eventually become ups.

Keep in mind that suicidal behavior is the result of a gradual wearing away of a person's self-image and ability to cope. Flunking an important test or being rejected by a boyfriend or girlfriend could be the last straw for a young person beset with many disappointments. There may also be major problems under the surface—the young person could be distraught over a death in the family or his parents' divorce, for example. It's not for you as a significant other to ferret out everything. That's the therapist's job. Just get the person talking about something and get him to a mental health professional, preferably one that has experience working with young people.

Youth: I'm just a big loser. My life's falling apart, but you couldn't understand.

If you're an older significant other, the young person may assume you're too old to understand. Try to put yourself in his place and show him you remember how you felt at that age. It could be helpful to relate a similar problem you experienced at the time. You might tell him you know how hard it is to be an adolescent.

> **You:** I do understand. Don't forget I was your age once. Being a teenager is not easy. I spent a lot of the time confused, and everything seemed to pile up. I didn't have much confidence that I could get things worked out or that I could fit in. I didn't get asked to my prom and it really hurt. I didn't want the other kids to see me as weird or different. But trust me, you can get over it. I did.

The same thing applies if you're a peer of the suicidal young person. An adolescent tends to think everyone else around him is doing great and he's the only one having trouble coping—a belief that can be reinforced by his peers' upbeat social media posts. The truth is, his peers probably also feel awkward to varying degrees, they're just embarrassed to talk about it. If you're the suicidal person's age, it's very important to let him know that other kids have troubles, too.

From an adult perspective, adolescence might seem a brief transition, while a young person may think he'll never get through this period. Ask him what he sees for himself a few years in the future. If he sees no future or the picture is bleak, try to get him to see something more optimistic.

> **Youth:** If my life is this screwed up now, it can only get worse as I get older. I'll never find someone to marry me. I'll be living in a grungy apartment all alone, working at some dumb treadmill job. I'll look back and the miserable time I'm having now in high school will be the high point of my life.

Try to help the youngster rebuild his self-esteem. You could point out the positives in his life—his accomplishments, special talents, and personality facets.

> **You:** I don't see it that way. You've got a lot going for you. You're attractive, and have a great sense of humor. And you couldn't be stupid and make the honor roll last semester.

Youth: But I must be totally crazy if I'm so depressed that I'm thinking about killing myself.

It's a good idea to assure the adolescent that he is perfectly normal, and that asking for help is the mark of a strong individual.

You: You're definitely not crazy! Depression happens to everybody.

Stress that depression can be treated and bad feelings will pass, while suicide is permanent.

You: You can get help for your depression. It may seem impossible to imagine now, but believe me, if you give it time, things will get better.
Youth: If I don't kill myself, they could get worse.
You: But they could get better. Why don't you give it a chance? I'll be glad to help you all I can.

Because of the decline of extended families and greater longevity in general, most young people today have not personally experienced the deaths of anyone they know. If they have, well-meaning parents often attempt to soften the blow by painting a romantic image of death, saying Grandma or Grandpa is an angel flying around up in heaven and having a wonderful time, for example. To an unhappy youth, this vision of dying can be very attractive.

The only experience many young people have with death is the uninvolving and griefless deaths in movies or on TV. In a medium in which a character can come back from the dead, or an actor who "died" on one program will show up on another, a young person may not understand the finality of death. He may see it as reversible.

Suicide may seem a way to achieve the love and attention that has eluded him in life. He may imagine that he'll reap the rewards somehow, witnessing his funeral, seeing his suicide's effect on friends, etc. Emphasize the realistic consequences of killing oneself.

You: If you kill yourself, what do you think will happen?

Youth: Well, everybody will come to my funeral and feel bad that they treated me the way they did. They'll be sorry and I'll be glad.

You: You'll never know if they're sorry. You'll be dead. More than likely, they'll be angry with you and think you did a foolish thing. No matter how bad things get, it's better to live.

Youth: Even like this?

You can offer some suggestions and volunteer to help in any way you can, but don't lecture or preach.

You: There are things you can do. You could ask someone to the prom yourself. It doesn't have to be anything romantic, you could just ask a friend. And I could quiz you for your next history test.

Youth: Yeah, I guess so. Sure.

Inquire about the young person's suicide plan. Remove any means the person could use to kill himself. Suggest seeking help from a mental health professional and make him promise not to harm himself until he sees a therapist. Keep tabs on the young person and help him fill his time until then. Follow through to make sure he is getting the help he needs.

If you think that the young person is in immediate danger, stay with him or call in someone else to stay with him—do not leave the person alone.

Parents must remember that everyone in the family is affected by the suicidal crisis and needs help in coping with it. No one person in the family is to blame, but everyone should be involved in the young person's recovery. Family therapy with as many family members as possible is recommended. The best safeguard against a young person's suicide is showing your unconditional love and keeping the lines of communication open.

As a non-parent significant other such as a member of the extended family, teacher, counselor, or family friend, you might feel reluctant to step on the parents' toes. Or you might figure that if there really is a problem, of course the parents would be taking care of it.

Keep in mind that some children are masters at hiding their true feelings, and are especially skillful where their families are concerned. In some cases, parents don't want to see a problem in the family and will deny it. Or they're simply too busy with other things to see the developing situation. Don't worry about overstepping your bounds. You could save a life.

If you are a peer dealing with a suicidal young person, don't take it all on your own shoulders. Get an adult involved. Talk to the person's parent or guardian. If the parent denies or minimizes the situation, go to another adult—a teacher, counselor, clergy, your own parents, the person's older brother or sister, etc.

Organize a group of friends to talk to the suicidal person and keep in touch with him. Peer counseling can be invaluable for him. All the other suggestions still apply: take the initiative with the suicidal young person, suggest that he sees a mental health professional, offer to accompany him when he sees the counselor, and make sure the person is not alone if the situation warrants. Let him know you care.

Most Importantly—Do not agree to keep your friend's suicidal intentions a secret.

Dealing with Suicide in the Schools

There is controversy over whether openly discussing suicide in schools and in the media is helpful. Some say it is dangerous and could possibly touch off further suicides. Studies show that suicidal behavior can influence young people who look to others as role models. Stories about suicide clusters of young people have come from all over the country. This phenomenon is hardly new. Goethe's *The Sufferings of Young Werther* triggered a youth suicide wave all over Europe after its publication in 1774.

But other experts believe that for every imitative suicide, many other young people could be helped by effective suicide discussion in the media and schools. Hopefully the contagion factor of suicide could be made to work the opposite way—perhaps more stories about successful public figures who at one time contemplated or attempted suicide but went on living could be inspirational to troubled people, young and old.

School is the ideal place to teach related issues such as how to utilize better coping skills and the availability of mental health resources. It's also the place to conduct anti-substance abuse and anti-bullying programs, two factors that can contribute to suicidal behavior.

Suicide prevention on a more intimate scale—setting up one-to-one counseling networks with peers, teachers, advisors, or staff—would probably be the most helpful. Creating an atmosphere in which students feel they can speak openly could head off trouble before it begins. What can keep suicidal people alive is the feeling of connectedness to someone or something outside of themselves. Although a young person may seem surrounded by classmates, friends, teachers, and family, he can still feel isolated and alienated.

Guidelines for Classroom Discussion

Young people are often reticent to speak about sensitive subjects such as suicide in front of a large group of people, so splitting up into smaller groups would probably be more helpful than holding large scale assemblies. You can have them write their questions anonymously on cards and have the moderator read and answer them aloud. Encourage the students to ask questions and try to conduct an open discussion.

1. Try to diffuse romantic notions of death and suicide. Emphasize that suicide is not *"Romeo and Juliet,"* but an avoidable waste of a life.

2. Stress the reality of killing oneself. Be direct, using words like "death" and "dying." Many young people think of dying as simply going to sleep. It never crosses their minds that it can be painful. Many also think they'll somehow be around to see the impact their deaths will have on others. Make it clear that they will not be able to reap the imagined rewards.

3. Give straightforward information on suicide and suicide prevention, emphasizing that the decision to commit

suicide is most likely not rational and usually does not come out of clear thinking or a noble purpose. Stress the fact that most suicidal people do not really want to die, but that they are attempting to cope with an intolerable situation in a manner which is nonconstructive. Suicidal people can learn to cope in better ways.

4. Allow the students to express their feelings. A question young people ask frequently is, "How do I know when the person is serious about suicide or is just trying to manipulate me?" Make it very clear that any suicidal statements, clues, or gestures should be taken seriously.

5. Keeping confidences is very important for young people. Stress that they should never promise to keep another's suicidal intentions a secret, and that they should alert others, particularly adults, that the suicidal young person is in danger.

6. Educate *against* suicide, not *about* it. Instead of concentrating on dying, talk about how to live better so that students don't become suicidal in the first place. Dwelling on the suicidal act itself can tend to romanticize it for a troubled young student.

7. Give the students information about available mental health resources in the community. Tell them, "If you're feeling down, it's okay to call the local mental health center," or "the suicide hotline," or "the peer counselor at school," etc. and give phone numbers and e-mail addresses. Young people may not be aware that such opportunities exist. They should also be made to feel secure that the services are confidential, and that they are not failures for using them.

8. Stress the facts about suicide and tell stories about others who were suicidal at one time, but are now happy they did not die.

Books and educational films on suicide are available for

schools. It's a good idea to ask a mental health professional who has handled suicides or another expert on the subject to speak to the class. You can contact the American Association of Suicidology's central office to locate members of the AAS Speakers/Writers Bureau Public Information Committee who would be available to speak and provide training.

Six

How Have Others Reached Out?

Stories of People Who Have Reached Out and Saved Loved Ones From Suicide

This chapter tells the stories of five significant others who have successfully reached out to a suicidal person. The experience was stressful for the significant others—all felt relatively high levels of anxiety. Additionally, all the relationships went through profound changes requiring some adjustments. But most important, the results were similarly positive—the suicidal person lived.

As a significant other, your goal is to keep the suicidal person alive and get him to professional help. Your first attempt to reach him may not go perfectly—it could take several tries. Use your knowledge of the suicidal person. Sensitivity, tact, and patience are important tools when discussing your concerns with him. Each situation will unfold differently, depending on the circumstances and your relationship.

The Story of a Young Significant Other

In light of the high youth suicide rate, a young person may find himself in the position of being a significant other for a suicidal peer. It is a difficult situation because as a young person, you usually have limited resources and are at a time in life when you may be inclined to reject adults and want to handle things on your own. It's important to realize that you must get a sympathetic adult involved. Another young life may depend on it.

Maddie and Lisa

Maddie and Lisa were both thirteen years old and best friends since elementary school. Lisa never got along with her stepmother, and life at home was bearable only because she was close to her father. When she was in middle school, he was in a serious auto accident—it was doubtful that he was going to make it. Lisa grew depressed and even started "cutting" herself on her arms, which can be seen as a suicidal gesture. Usually talkative, she became quieter in class, quit after-school activities, and stopped going to church.

One night, Lisa called Maddie in tears. She was upset about the latest in a long succession of fights with her stepmother. She talked to Maddie about other bad things that had happened to her, such as being rejected by a boy she liked, flunking a class, and the usual turmoil in her family.

Midway through the two-hour conversation, Lisa hinted at suicide. Maddie was stunned—she would never think of Lisa as someone who would become suicidal. Lisa was "everyone's comedian." Initially, Maddie thought that she was blowing things out of proportion, but she couldn't get Lisa out of her depressed mood. Lisa was home alone and when she started reading off the labels on her father's prescriptions, Maddie got seriously scared and briefly thought about calling the police or an ambulance. She didn't, nor did she consider telling her parents, because at that stage of her life, she thought they would be more of a hinderance than a help.

At one point Lisa said, "It would be much easier to get this whole thing over with. You know, just walk off a bridge or something." Maddie now says, "At first, I got angry and told Lisa that she was being selfish and that she was hurting me, but that just got her angrier. That's when she got hysterical and started screaming, 'I could do it right here.'"

Maddie unwittingly challenged Lisa by telling her, "You can't do this. You can't kill yourself." Lisa's automatic response was, "Yes, I can." She went on to say, "It really doesn't matter and you can't tell me not to."

Naturally, in this situation, one possible first reaction of a significant other is to be frightened and angry, but it's important to remain calm and think it through before saying anything. Maddie realized she was getting nowhere and changed her tack. She said the most important thing she could say to Lisa—how the suicide would affect Maddie.

"I kept telling her that she couldn't leave me and that we needed to talk about it. I didn't try to tell her, 'Your parents love you, your family cares about you,' because I didn't think that's what she wanted to hear. I told her over and over again that she was my best friend and that I loved her and that I needed her to be around. That if she left me, I wouldn't know what to do." That seemed to turn the tide.

Maddie told Lisa that she wanted to come over, but there was no one at home to drive her and it was too far to walk, and she couldn't talk on her cell phone while riding her bike to Lisa's. Maddie says, "I felt like it was really urgent that I be where she was, but I didn't feel like I could get off the phone with her."

Finally, Lisa stopped crying and they started talking about what they were going to do the next week. When Maddie thought that she had gotten Lisa calm enough, she told her to sit down in her bedroom and watch TV. Maddie rode her bike over to Lisa's as fast as she could and found her doing just what she had told her to do.

Giving Lisa specific instructions was very helpful—the person in crisis needs someone supportive to be in charge of his life temporarily while he himself can't be. This is not a permanent position and the relationship must get back into balance later when the suicidal person is stable. Tell him, for example, "I'm on my way over" and give him something diverting to do—reading, playing piano, doing housework—

which will keep him busy until you get there.

Not wanting to be around when Lisa's stepmother came home, they walked down to the beach where they often hung out. Maddie noticed that Lisa kept her long sleeved jacket on even though it was a nice sunny day, but she didn't mention it. That night, Maddie had Lisa sleep over at her house. Getting Lisa out of the hostile environment at home, and keeping an eye on her that night, was a good idea on Maddie's part.

The next day, Lisa didn't want to eat. She and Maddie discussed everything but her problems, which Maddie now acknowledges was a mistake. "She didn't want to talk about it, so I just sort of let it go. Knowing what I know now, I would have made her talk about it, but at the time I was afraid. I also would have pressed her about why she didn't take off her jacket at the beach. I found out later that she'd been 'cutting' her arms and was hiding it."

"Cutting" may be an effort to cope with intense anxiety and may not be a suicide attempt, however it should be seen as a suicidal gesture. As such, "cutting" is sometimes dismissed as an attempt to get attention, but this behavior should be taken seriously and needs to be evaluated by a mental health professional.

It's understandable that both girls were reluctant to talk about Lisa's suicidal episode. The suicidal person may not want to bring it up because he is embarrassed, doesn't want to scare the significant other again, or feels that he's being a burden. The significant other may fear that "reminding" the person of his suicidal feelings will reignite them, may not want to pry, or may think it's unnecessary unless the suicidal person brings it up first.

But, as a significant other, you must reinforce your interest in the suicidal person and encourage him to open up if he needs to. You should simply ask, "How are you doing?" If the suicidal person says something innocuous, such as, "Fine," you should ask candidly, "I'm still concerned about you. Are you suicidal?"

Getting adults involved is one of the most important things that you as a young significant other can do. Just as you may assume that a teenager has more maturity and experience than a preschooler, you must realize that an older person has more than you. If there is no adult that you feel comfortable approaching, go directly to a professional, be it your family doctor, the school nurse, the local mental health center, a suicide prevention center, or a private therapist. Do not attempt to deal with this on your own.

Maddie didn't consider getting Lisa's father involved because he was so ill. She and Lisa were worried about taxing him too much. "I think he would have loved to have done anything, but he wasn't in the position where he could have. And we were at a time in life when the people you counted on were your friends and you didn't go much further than that." Maddie suggested to Lisa that she discuss her problems with a counselor at school whom they liked, but didn't press it when Lisa said no.

It would have been better had Maddie then talked to the counselor herself, but at least she spoke with another friend in their group, Pam. Unbeknownst to Lisa, they agreed to keep an eye on her. Pam's mother was one of the few adults they found easy to talk with, so they told her about it. She wanted to contact Lisa's stepmother. The girls balked, arguing that her stepmother would discount the whole thing, besides, Lisa seemed okay now.

Pam's mother did contact a teacher at school, who talked to Lisa about the situation at home and told her that he was available anytime she needed to discuss her problems. Lisa mentioned their conversation to Maddie—she said it made her feel better and suggested that if Maddie ever needed to, this teacher was a good person to talk with.

As Lisa's father got better, her depression lifted and she recovered her sense of humor. "In a couple of months, she was back to the same person that she was before all this happened," remembers Maddie. "She was the one person who didn't have the major breakdowns in friendships during high school, and didn't have serious problems in school."

Maddie supposes that if the situation had gone on and Lisa hadn't gotten better so soon, she would have mentioned it to Lisa's father, despite his health problems. A very important thing she did was to make sure that Lisa had a lot of support among their circle of friends. If Lisa couldn't go out, Maddie would go over to her house and spend time with her, or bring the whole group over to Lisa's.

As with the suicidal episodes of many young people, Maddie believes that Lisa wasn't thinking in terms of dying. "At first, I think it was, 'Things are so bad, I can't handle it anymore.' I believe she thought that she'd lost her dad. I don't think she was thinking that when you die, you're gone. I think it was more like, 'This will get rid of the pain.'"

She speculates that one of the reasons Lisa didn't kill herself was her uncertainty of what happens after death. "She wasn't sure that God was going to be there to hold her hand and take her into the light or whatever. I think that one of the things that stopped Lisa was the total fear that she had no idea what was waiting for her."

In the past, Maddie would go to Lisa with her problems, but with this experience, they switched roles. "She was definitely my anchor. Then I guess I became her emotional anchor. It was really weird when she stopped being my support and needed it herself. Before this, Lisa looked out for me. After that, I felt like I had to watch out for her. And she let me."

Lisa was lucky that she had such a devoted friend in Maddie and that her father recovered. If a person can garner enough emotional support and the situation which made him suicidal changes, he can recover without professional counseling, as Lisa was able to do. (Counseling could have helped the difficult relationship with her stepmother, which was an ongoing major problem for her, though.) On the other hand, if her father hadn't recovered, she could have remained depressed and suicidal. It is best in every case to at least get brief counseling from a mental health professional.

Getting Other Significant Others Involved

Forming a network of support for the suicidal person is very important, but telling other significant others about your concerns may be difficult. Broach the subject in much the same way as you would with the suicidal person himself. Open with "I" statements, such as, "I am concerned about Mary." Then go into examples of why you are concerned—"Mary hasn't seemed to recover from her miscarriage. She's very depressed and cries all the time. Lately, she's been telling me that she has nothing to live for anymore. I'm worried that she might be considering suicide."

If the other people are receptive, carefully plan your next moves. Decide who would be the best one to approach the suicidal person. Determine if it is more helpful for you to approach him together, or whether he will feel like you're "ganging up" on him. If you decide that only one person should talk to him, those in the support network should be in the background, ready to step in if they are needed.

Amanda and Mitch

Mitch's parents were farmers, but it had been a losing proposition for the past four years. This season, the entire crop was wiped out and they were about to lose their farm, their home, everything. In their early fifties, they felt that they were too old to start a new business. They'd been somewhat down for the past four years, but now Mitch's father would sit with his head in his hands, talking about how depressed he was. Mitch's mother began talking about suicide.

At first, Mitch thought his mother was just being manipulative and was more worried about his father being suicidal. However, his wife Amanda became concerned that her mother-in-law was seriously considering killing herself. "I kept thinking I was crazy, that I was reading too much into the situation," says Amanda. "I can't remember any particular thing that let me know. It was more of an intuition."

During one visit, Mitch's mother had sorted out family mementos into different stacks for each of her three children. Mitch and Amanda were afraid that she was making out her will and preparing for death, but both parents seemed to be in good moods for a change. Mitch and Amanda backed off, confused by their pleasantness.

"It was the best visit we'd had with them in a year. They were cheerful... even seemed optimistic," remembers Mitch. "Everybody had been so afraid. We'd say, 'We need to confront this, say the word "suicide," and talk about everything.' And we went up and things looked fine."

Amanda felt her suspicions were correct, but she didn't know how to bring them up with her in-laws. "I didn't want

The Suicide Dilemma

to be blasé and say, 'Yeah, I know how you feel, but cheer up,' because we haven't lost everything. We can say to them, 'You ought to try this and this,' but because Mitch is the baby of the family and I'm an outsider, I didn't think they'd listen."

Amanda realized that sometimes, the significant other who is the closest to the suicidal person isn't necessarily the best candidate to speak to him. It may be critical to find another significant other that the suicidal person will listen to, be it the person's spouse, relative, teacher, or clergyman. Don't let egos get involved. The main thing is to get the suicidal person to open up.

Mitch and Amanda called a friend of the family, Sam, to whom they thought their parents would listen. Sam was closer in age to them and could relate to their problems, having suffered major financial setbacks of his own. Sam immediately confronted Mitch's parents.

He told Mitch's dad, "I feel like you're considering suicide." Mitch's dad pointed to his wife and said, "No, not me. Her." Sam jumped on it. "He was real graphic and blunt about death and suicide, which is what was needed," says Amanda. He asked Mitch's mother how she planned to do it and she admitted she had three ideas—overdosing on sleeping pills, wrecking the car, or shooting herself. Sam got her to promise him that she would not commit suicide, but he felt she needed to make that promise to her son as well.

After Sam talked to Mitch's parents, Mitch and Amanda spoke with them. "It was like being part of a dream, or being a character in a story," reports Mitch. "I kept saying to myself, 'This is real. You're awake, this is happening.' It was a real tense situation and my stomach was in knots." Mitch's mother promised him that she would not commit suicide. The following Sunday at church, she stood up and confessed to the whole congregation that she'd been considering suicide. The church community rallied around her and pledged its support.

It may take a lot of convincing for some significant others to understand that a problem exists. They may not have picked up on the same clues you have. Or they may realize that there is a problem, but are denying it for whatever reason. Be persistent. If you finally reach a point where you figure it's no use, don't feel like you've failed. At least you have alerted another significant other to the problem. Perhaps he'll come around later. If on the other hand, the person agrees with your assessment of the situation, but feels too uncomfortable to help you, don't push him. Someone who is ill-at-ease may be more of a detriment than an asset. Just ask if you can call upon him if you need to.

Understand that others may not have the knowledge about suicide that you now have. Getting them to read books or websites about suicide is one way to educate them. Be sure to dispel any myths they may have about suicide. Make sure they know what to do in case of a suicide attempt. Do not scare them, and try to instill hope that the suicidal person can be helped. Always stress that suicide is preventable and depression is treatable.

Make sure the significant others in the support network know how to reach each other twenty-four hours a day. Keep each other posted on the developments in the suicidal person's situation. Explain that if they have any questions about dealing with the suicidal person, they should consult a mental health professional.

When You Are the Most Significant Significant Other

You may find that you are the only significant other that the suicidal person will confide in. This is a difficult situation that should be avoided, since the suicidal person is putting you into the same position as a therapist. Do not let the suicidal person convince you that you are the only person who can help him. This can deplete your energy and limit your resources for helping the suicidal person. It is important to get as many people involved as possible.

However, if the suicidal person focuses on you and refuses to listen to others, make sure that you have people giving you support. Your support network should include a mental health professional who can advise you on how to deal with the suicidal person, as well as with your own anxieties.

Michael and Elizabeth

Michael, a keyboard player in a struggling band, was having one of "those" days. The band had just gotten a gig as the opening act for a major group, but at the last minute, their drummer quit. As Michael was desperately trying to find a replacement, his ex-wife Elizabeth called him in tears. She angrily hung up on him when his call waiting system beeped with another call.

Michael called her right back. Elizabeth said she was completely overwhelmed by problems. Unable to stand her job anymore, she had impulsively quit and was now facing eviction because she couldn't pay the rent. In addition, her apartment had been broken into. The ordeal left her feeling very shaken and vulnerable, and now she was having trouble dealing with her insurance company. The last straw was a looming deadline on her doctoral thesis. She had fallen behind because of a minor illness during the semester and didn't think she could finish it in time.

Adding to her sense of frustration with herself was the knowledge that normally she could have handled these problems, but she was having trouble now because they occurred all at once. For the first time in her life, she wanted to kill herself and was very frightened. So was Michael.

"I was scared and didn't know how to handle the situation, plus I had a conflict because I had work to take care of," says Michael. "I was running around trying to get ready to go on the road. It was probably the busiest couple of days I'd had in a long time. And here she was needing my help. I had to take it seriously. I was having to make a decision over what to do with my career versus taking care of her."

Despite his professional obligations, he kept her on the phone for an hour or two, talking her out of suicide. When he asked about her plans, Elizabeth said she wanted to overdose on pills. Fortunately, her roommate had arranged an appointment for her with a psychotherapist. Before the conversation ended, Michael talked with the roommate and verified that she would take Elizabeth to the therapist's office.

Although he knew that his ex-wife was dating another man at the time, Elizabeth made it clear to Michael that he was the only person she could trust. "She made me responsible," says Michael, who admits he didn't like being put into that situation, but still had feelings for her. He suspected that she might have been doing this to try to get him to come back to her, but says, "I had to take it seriously. Whether or not it was manipulative, I still had to follow through."

There is no foolproof litmus test to determine whether the suicidal person is really in trouble or simply trying to manipulate you. It is a question that you may often ask yourself in frustration, particularly if the situation goes on for a long time, or if the suicidal person seems to focus solely on you. Even if the person is being manipulative, it doesn't mean he isn't in distress. Since you can't read his mind, all you can do is observe his behavior and operate on what he tells you. If he says he's going to kill himself, you have no choice but to take his threats seriously.

Michael could have washed his hands of the situation once he learned that Elizabeth's roommate was looking out for her. However, he followed up the next day and discovered that although Elizabeth was not to be left alone (per the therapist's orders), the roommate had left the apartment. Elizabeth disappeared, panicking everybody. Michael talked to the roommate and realized that the situation was too much of an emotional strain on her—she was shutting down. It looked like Elizabeth's support system was falling apart and that Michael would have to fill the void. "Elizabeth had a lot of ambivalence about killing herself and was looking for people who would restrain her," says Michael. "Which is why she contacted several people, all of whom failed her, except me."

Although he was supposed to leave town with the band, he decided to delay the trip one night and went over to Elizabeth's. Michael joked with her to see if she still had her sense of humor and was pleased to note that somehow she was even able to laugh about her present situation. But towards the end of the evening, Elizabeth became upset because she thought he was going to abandon her. She said several times, "Don't leave me. You're my last hope."

When she asked if he was going away, Michael was honest and told her he was. Elizabeth became very upset. "You're going to leave me. Everyone does," she cried. Michael answered, "Yes, I have to, I can't do this forever. But I'll stay with you tonight and talk to you as long as you want."

The conversation didn't start out well. Michael wasn't sure what to say and resorted to standard adages, such as,

"Don't let this get you down. You're more important than any silly term paper," which trivialized one of the things that was making her feel suicidal. Elizabeth became increasingly hostile, raging at one point, "No one listens to me!" and she stopped talking. Michael realized that she was right—he had just been telling her what he thought she wanted to hear. He asked, "Why don't you think I'm listening?" but she wouldn't answer. Michael persisted, asking the question over and over again.

Finally, Elizabeth opened up. Michael understood that she didn't need to get reassurance of everybody's love and concern—that wasn't going to change the situation which had caused her depression. In the first case in this chapter, what worked for Maddie was telling Lisa how much she meant to her, but Elizabeth needed practical help getting through her problems—especially the problem with finishing her thesis.

As a significant other, you must be flexible and willing to try different ways to reach the suicidal person if you initially run into an impasse. Listen to what he is saying. Do not ignore the obvious—the person may be reacting to circumstances that, with a little help, are not beyond his control. Perhaps he cannot see the solution himself. A person may be experiencing situational depression because he is overwhelmed by some practical problem in life. By attempting to alleviate that problem, you can sometimes ease a situation which is contributing to the depression.

For example, if someone is depressed about his job, do what you can to help him find another one. If he is depressed about his apartment, help him find another place to live. If a student is depressed about flunking a class, find him a tutor. In a case in which someone is depressed about a loved one who has died, obviously you cannot bring back the dead, but you can help the suicidal person cope with the loss, get involved in other activities, and go on with his life. Another example is a person who is suicidal at the end of a relationship that has no chance of being resumed, or is so detrimental it should not be resumed. You can help the suicidal person get focused on other activities.

Michael arranged to catch up with the band later, and worked with Elizabeth all night and the next two days. "She had her ups and downs, but she got the stuff done. At the end of that time, we left things pretty stable. What helped was that I physically got her through this crisis by helping her with her thesis and by helping her write the necessary letters to her insurance company about the robbery. She was no longer overwhelmed and was beginning to feel that she could deal with things," says Michael. After that, he eased himself out of the day to day, although he kept in touch with her. Elizabeth eventually resumed her activities and gratefully credited Michael with saving her life.

Michael handled the situation well, despite the ambiguity of his relationship with Elizabeth, which made it difficult for him to determine what was expected of him at first. The situation made him understandably resentful of the demands that Elizabeth made on him.

As the significant other, you must be self-defining and set your own limits, gently telling the suicidal person what you will and will not do. For example, "I can stay with you tonight, but tomorrow, I have to go to work." Make sure the suicidal person will not be left alone, asking him, "Since I can't stay with you all the time, who else is acceptable?" If the suicidal person names someone, arrange a schedule to make sure that person is with him when you are gone.

If the suicidal person becomes upset and gives you an ultimatum, "If you leave, I'll kill myself," calmly tell him, "I have to leave, I can't stay with you forever. Since I don't want you to hurt yourself, you leave me with very few alternatives. I can hospitalize you, arrange for someone else to stay with you while I'm out, or we can go talk to a therapist together. But we have to do something." Let the suicidal person help you choose between the three options. Elizabeth opted to see a therapist, so Michael made an appointment and went with her to the first session. Michael felt that Elizabeth and the therapist made a good connection, so he left for the tour, but still kept tabs on her.

If you find yourself in the position of being the only significant other, you must get a professional involved as your consultant immediately. Call a suicide crisis line, a mental health center, a private therapist—but **do not try to handle this on your own.** It is important to be honest with the suicidal person. Tell him that you are consulting with someone, but do it in such a way that you don't seem to be rejecting him. You can say, "I'm really worried about you. I think I need help so I'm consulting with a professional." If the suicidal person gets upset because he imagines you will be talking about him, tell him, "Yes, it's likely that we will be talking about you. Let's make an appointment and we'll both talk to the therapist together."

When Hospitalization Is Necessary

Sometimes a suicidal person will need more than you or an outpatient therapist can give him, and admission to a hospital is necessary. Many suicidal people admit they have a problem and go voluntarily. But if the suicidal person refuses, or is so incapacitated that he is unable make a decision, an involuntary commitment to hospitalization may be necessary. It is one of the toughest decisions a significant other may have to face and you should always consult with a mental health professional to help you decide the best course of action to take.

Hannah and Margaret

Hannah's mother, Margaret, was in her sixties, retired and widowed. She became depressed when Hannah and her husband built a new house and moved quite a distance away from her. At around the same time, the dog she'd had for nearly fifteen years died. It was devastating for her. Margaret got to a point where she stayed home constantly, and even became so paranoid that she stopped going to the door for fear that someone was coming to hurt her.

One night, Margaret called Hannah and told her that she was leaving. Hannah asked where she was going and she said that she was going to die. Hannah asked, "Why did you say that?" and her mother answered that she had taken some sleeping pills.

"I didn't realize that she had gotten that bad, because we were so involved in building the house. She would cover it up when I was with her," remembers Hannah.

Hannah called 9-1-1, and the paramedics agreed to meet

her at her mother's house. Neither Hannah nor the paramedics were able to determine the number of pills Margaret had taken, but Hannah told them that her mother seemed completely in another world. The paramedics transported Margaret to the local ER, where the doctors determined that Margaret was not in physical danger, but admitted her overnight for observation. Hannah stayed with her mother all night at the hospital.

"It was really devastating. I guess I was feeling very guilty because I had pushed my mother aside when we were building the house," says Hannah.

The following morning, Margaret expressed regret about taking the pills and stated that she did not want to die. Hannah consulted with her rabbi, who suggested taking Margaret to a mental health center, so Hannah made an appointment that day.

The therapist said that Margaret needed extensive therapy and suggested that she be committed to a hospital. Hannah resisted, certain that her mother would improve on her own. The next day, her mother grew more irrational, imagining that bugs were crawling on her. This really frightened Hannah. "I had never dealt with anyone like that. I didn't know what to do. Mother wasn't capable of making decisions at that point either. Being an only child, it was all up to me to make those choices and I knew she was ill."

The decision whether to hospitalize a loved one can be agonizing, one that the significant other may try to avoid for fear of incurring the anger of the suicidal person and others concerned. A significant other might be hesitant to hospitalize a suicidal loved one because he fears that he is trampling on the suicidal person's individual rights. These misapprehensions must be put on hold while the suicidal person is a danger to himself.

Do not leave it solely up to the suicidal person as to whether or not he should be hospitalized. If the person is rational, you may include him in the decision-making process, but do not give him veto power. He is probably not making the best decisions at this point—if he was thinking clearly, he wouldn't be suicidal in the first place. Keep in mind that he needs you to tell him what to do—it can lower his anxiety level if someone takes control. In most situations, you must assume a nearly parental role in the relationship with the suicidal person. This role can be especially difficult when the significant other is the child of the suicidal person, as in Hannah's case.

The next night, after discussing it with a psychotherapist, Hannah went to the magistrate's office and filled out the forms for committing Margaret. Hannah broke down when she had to tell the magistrate what her mother had done to hurt herself. "I remember sitting there, crying so hard. It's still painful when I think about it today," remembers Hannah.

She took her mother to the county hospital to be examined by the emergency room doctor, who then signed the papers for commitment. "I explained to her what we were doing and why it was necessary. She was fine; she agreed. It was like dealing with a child. That wasn't a problem. But even knowing I was doing the best for Mother, I couldn't help but feel like I was betraying her. The magistrate tried to explain that this is what needed to be done. He said, 'Even though it's painful, in the long run your mother will be better for it.' In that respect, he was 100% correct."

Margaret was in the hospital nine days, which she and Hannah believe was very beneficial—for both of them. "It gave Mother a chance to level off. They put her on antidepressants and got her to the point where she was stable," says Hannah. "She received therapy and made some good friends, which was also very helpful." The stay provided Hannah the breathing space she needed in order to figure out what to do with her mother.

When Margaret got out of the hospital, Hannah moved in with her for two days and recalls, "It was a very trying time. The money situation was tight for her and for me, too. Never having had to deal with anything like this all by myself, it was extremely emotional. I now had my mother to take care of."

Margaret's sister came to stay for a couple of days as well. During that time, Hannah checked into placing her mother into an intensive day treatment program at the local community mental health center, which consisted of both individual and group therapy.

Margaret agreed it was the right thing to do, and she participated in the intensive day treatment program for two months.

After approximately three weeks, she began to improve. The medicine started taking effect and, being a gregarious person, Margaret began to make friends in the program.

At the end of the two months, Hannah talked to Margaret about selling her house and moving in with her, but Margaret wanted to stay in her house and try being by herself.

Hannah reports that her mother got back into an active life and has been fine ever since. "She has a dog now, and he and her grandchildren are the main things in her life. She's now actively involved in a senior citizen's club most days and volunteers at the local library. She is constantly doing something. That time when she was suicidal was bad for her, but it ended up being good in the long run. I'm really proud of her."

Effects on Significant Others

Often, when a significant other can stick with someone and help him through a suicidal crisis, he feels that he has accomplished something. The bond between the two may deepen and open up communication for a better relationship. Being there and helping a loved one can provide a great satisfaction for the significant other.

On the other hand, a significant other may also find that dealing with a suicidal person can be a very stressful, draining experience. He may feel a variety of emotions, from fear and anxiety, to resentment and frustration. Some significant others even need counseling themselves to help them get through this trying time. If you find yourself having difficulties dealing with the situation, don't hesitate to get professional help—you can't help the suicidal person if you're having problems yourself.

It is very common to have feelings of guilt over failing the suicidal person or possibly being the catalyst for their suicidal state. Hannah felt that everything was her fault because she had neglected her mother. She remembers, "I felt very sorry and sad, like I had let her down. I felt very guilty because I hadn't paid her as much attention as I had before." Hannah should not feel responsible though—a combination of factors lead to a person's feeling suicidal. She also felt a great deal of guilt over having to hospitalize her mother, even though she believed it was the right thing to do and was ultimately proved right by her mother's recovery.

Anger is also a very common feeling. Michael remembers, "I felt some anger and resentment. I didn't like being put in that situation. We were divorced, but Elizabeth was coming back to me for help when we had long ago cut our romantic ties. I thought, 'Why can't she take care of the situation?' But I let go of whatever anger I felt because I cared about her and knew she needed my help."

Be careful not to vent the anger on the suicidal person and appear as though you are rejecting him. If you begin to resent the suicidal person, that is your signal that you need to take a break and should get more support. Resenting the person is not going to benefit the situation. Find a release for your anger by talking to other people.

Dealing with a person with psychological problems can be frustrating. With a physical illness, you can see that the person is sick and you have some idea about what to expect. Also, because all suicidal people are ambivalent, you may receive mixed signals from him. It is common as a significant other to feel manipulated and resentful—and guilty about those feelings. Not knowing whether someone is truly suicidal can be frustrating, but try looking at it positively as the manifestation of the suicidal person's own uncertainty about whether to kill himself.

Daniel and Nancy

There is a danger of getting too caught up in the situation. Some significant others may develop problems due to the stress of dealing with a suicidal loved one, particularly if they have other pressures to contend with.

Daniel wasn't sleeping or eating. His counselor at school called his mother Nancy several times, complaining that he couldn't sit still in class. For a period of five days, he seemed unusually energetic and driven, becoming obsessed with the idea that he could become a stockbroker. He decided to open his own firm, renting and furnishing an expensive apartment for an office. It would have been an ambitious scheme even for an adult, but Daniel was only seventeen. All the checks he had written to finance the venture bounced, and everything came to a head when the police became involved.

At first, drugs were suspected, but Nancy took Daniel to a psychiatrist who diagnosed him as having bipolar disorder. For Nancy, it was the climax to years of feeling that Daniel had serious problems. Friends and family had always talked her out of it, but this time nobody could deny it.

For Nancy, simply getting the diagnosis was beneficial. "I was relieved when I found out that something was wrong with Daniel because I'd had problems with him ever since he was a young child. At least now I knew what was wrong. I thought I had been crazy all these years. People told me I didn't know what I was talking about. Knowing that that was going on, I could accept it and deal with it."

Unfortunately, the medication prescribed for Daniel made his symptoms worse. He would become much higher during his manic phases and lower when depressed. During one manic phase, Nancy had to hospitalize him for ten days.

When he cycled back into depression, he ran his car into a streetlight, but luckily avoided serious injury. He told his girlfriend that he had tried to kill himself and she told his mother. "I think he became suicidal when he felt that his life was totally out of control, and that he wasn't going to get any better. He felt that there was no hope," says Nancy.

Since Daniel didn't react well to his previous experience in the hospital and he was under a therapist's care, Nancy kept him at home. She never left Daniel alone during this period. "You have to make sure that there is no way they can hurt themselves. I knew if he'd been given half an opportunity, he definitely would have tried to kill himself. He felt that there was no reason to live."

Daniel was very difficult to deal with and his illness began taking its toll on them both. Says Nancy, "When I was scraping him off the roof when he was manic, I would wish he was in a depressed state. When he was depressed and suicidal, I would give anything to have him back manic. I felt as if the illness was driving both of us insane."

"I was very, very frightened. And then I was angry, for a long time. And sorry for myself. It wasn't fair that I had this enormous burden to deal with."

Nancy also felt guilty because she believed the illness was genetic in origin. It is quite common for parents to feel overly responsible when their child becomes suicidal. As a parent of a suicidal child, don't waste energy worrying over things you can't do anything about, such as having passed on an unfortunate gene or having made a possible mistake in child-rearing. Concentrate on getting the suicidal person to professional help. Remember that suicide is the result of many influences and that young people can become suicidal even in the most stable of family situations.

The crisis with Daniel couldn't have happened at a worse time for Nancy. She had other serious problems in her life—she was unemployed, with no prospects of finding a job. In addition, a long-term relationship was falling apart, and her other child was having problems as well. "It was without a doubt, the lowest period of my life. I had tremendous feelings of failure in all areas. There were days I just didn't know how I was going to make it. I felt that death was inevitable. I almost thought it would be better if he could just die some other way, at least he couldn't commit suicide. It's a terrible thing. I just remember feeling that there was no way out."

Nancy became suicidal herself. This can be disastrous. The significant other cannot help the suicidal person if he himself is depressed and suicidal. He should seek professional help immediately, and find others to help look after the suicidal person.

Nancy started seeing her therapist every day and promised, out of respect for her, that she wouldn't do anything to hurt herself. She brought Daniel to a psychiatrist who conducted extensive tests on him to determine the proper medication.

Daniel started responding to the new medicine and for nearly two weeks, didn't have a severe mood distortion. "Life did start to get better," says Nancy. She found joining a support group for parents of mentally ill children very beneficial. "I learned that I had to keep myself separate from the illness, in order to not become as sick as Daniel was. Which is a very hard thing to do, especially when it's your child. That took me quite a while."

The important thing as a significant other is to not go beyond your own endurance. It may be hard to recognize your limit because you are so caught up in caring for the suicidal person. It may also be hard to admit your limit because you feel such a responsibility to help the suicidal person. But be sure to take care of yourself or you won't be able to take care of him.

Picking Up the Pieces

A suicidal episode can profoundly affect your relationship with another person. Even if it affects it negatively, just keep in mind that it's better to make someone very angry at you than to lose him to suicide.

As the suicidal person improves and regains some control over his life, you will need to relinquish the parental role. Professional counseling may be necessary to help the relationship regain its balance, which may take some time. It is important to not reject the suicidal person and to not make a decision about your relationship in the immediate aftermath of a suicidal crisis. It is best to stay in the relationship and to give it a chance to work out. As no relationship is perfect, look at this as a good opportunity to make some needed changes.

You may find a big difference in the way the suicidal person reacts to you. He might be grateful to you for saving his life, or at the other extreme, he might feel betrayed, angry, and resentful towards you for thwarting his wishes. He may also be embarrassed that you saw him at his lowest point. Or he may feel closer to you for having gone through such an intimate experience together.

In Michael's case, he reports, "Elizabeth was very adamant in her praise of me. She's credited me many times with being the person who saved her life." But, he could see that she was interested in picking up the romance. Although he wasn't completely adverse to that, he nonetheless felt a great deal of conflict. He couldn't help but feel she had manipulated him and was angry that he'd had to put his career at risk. The main thing was that from now on, he felt that his view of her would be negatively affected by what had happened.

Says Michael, "People sometimes think, 'Maybe I'd be better off dead,' but I've never given into that, why has she? I know that's unfair, but on some level, I know that I see it that way. I find myself saying, on the other hand, she had every right to be in the state she was in, because anyone else under those stresses would have felt just the same way." It is important for a significant other to be as understanding as possible and to try to see things from the suicidal person's perspective, as Michael was able to do.

Since the situation was so difficult for him, Michael confided in a couple of his fellow band members and now worries that they will see Elizabeth as unstable and a potential problem for him if he resumes a long-term relationship with her. "I don't know what I want to do, but I don't want this incident to prevent me from having a relationship that might be a good one. And who knows, it might." Michael joined Elizabeth in couples therapy to work it out.

In some cases, once the suicidal person is receiving therapy and the situation has stabilized, the suicidal person may withdraw from the significant other for a while, seeking out new acquaintances who know nothing about his suicidal episode. He may do this out of embarrassment from appearing needy or in an effort to prove to the significant other that he is strong again and doesn't need him anymore. It may be helpful to allow a cooling-off period at this point—particularly if there is a lot of anger on the part of either the suicidal person or the significant other.

Both Nancy and Daniel were very angry with each other. Nancy was upset because Daniel refused to allow her to join him in family therapy, while Daniel felt that Nancy was too controlling. When Daniel recovered enough to be able to go away to college, Nancy was happy for both their sakes. "I'm very relieved to be away from the situation on a day in, day out basis."

"I think it will take some more time. We have a lot of anger with each other, and keeping a distance is probably the best thing right now," says Nancy. "I'll always be there and I'll always take care of him, and he knows that, but I'm exhausted from it. We're both going to have to sit down and really let it all hang out. Hopefully, someday, we will be close again." Nancy retreated in order not to put any more pressure on their relationship, but is keeping the door open for the time when Daniel is ready to step back in.

On the other hand, some suicidal people and significant others feel a deep bond after having gone through the experience. Although Maddie felt the need to start looking out for Lisa following her suicidal episode, there was never any awkwardness between them. "We always had a really open relationship. That never changed," remembers Maddie.

Although now, nearly ten years later, Maddie and Lisa don't see each other quite so often, they still have a special feeling for each other. "We've stuck it out as friends for a pretty long time. It's not the kind of thing you normally deal with while growing up. I don't know anybody else who felt like they were going to lose their best friend. I was scared to death."

Hannah and her mother, Margaret, became closer as well. For many years before, they hadn't really talked. Hannah withheld a lot from Margaret because she felt that her mother couldn't handle it. Margaret was unable to talk with her daughter openly and honestly as an adult.

During the suicidal episode, as Hannah and her mother made decisions together about how to reorganize her life, they were forced to break down the barriers. Family counseling helped them practice communication skills which improved their relationship. Later, when Hannah experienced marital problems, she confided in her mother for the first time in years.

"During all that I've been through lately, she's been there for me," says Hannah. "All those years before, I've babied her and never told her anything, but now she's helpful to me. I think it makes her feel better about herself, too."

None of these interventions went perfectly, but all came out well—the suicidal person lived. Each significant other made some mistakes along the way, but the most important thing they did was hanging in there. They let the suicidal person know that he or she was important to them and that they cared. That's what makes the difference.

Seven

Treating the Suicidal Person

The Treatment and Recovery Process, and How You Can Help

Developments in psychotherapy and antidepressants make it possible for the suicidal person to recover and return to his life. This section outlines ways in which you can find help for the person, what to expect in the treatment process, and how you can be supportive in his recovery.

Finding Treatment When the Situation Is Not an Emergency

Finding a mental health professional can be a relatively stressful experience for the family of a suicidal person. In most cases, the family is in the midst of a crisis and is very anxious and upset.

When someone is suicidal, but not in imminent danger (the person may be having suicidal thoughts but has not made a plan or a suicide attempt), if you don't know a mental health professional to call, get in touch with your primary care provider or community mental health center for a referral. It is a good idea to gather as many referrals as possible.

Due to the need for confidentiality, mental health professionals cannot give you a list of satisfied customers to call. However, if you happen to know people who were treated by that therapist, ask their opinion. If they have any complaints or were dissatisfied, ask them to be specific. Do not reject a therapist on the basis of one person's opinion, but bear his comments in mind.

Community mental health centers are generally the most affordable treatment options. Many community mental health centers offer a range of treatment programs including individual and group psychotherapy, outpatient drug and alcohol rehabilitation programs, and access to evaluation for medications.

Obtaining Treatment in Emergency Situations

If the suicidal person is threatening to kill himself (either verbally or in writing), has a plan, or has made a suicide attempt, inpatient treatment may be necessary. If the person has attempted suicide, call 9-1-1 immediately. If the suicide attempter has received medical treatment, but does not need a medical admission to the hospital, have someone stay with him until you decide on inpatient or outpatient treatment for him. This decision should be made only after consultation with medical and mental health professionals. Talk to the staff psychiatrist if the hospital has one. Your local hospital may even have an inpatient treatment program.

Inpatient Treatment

Inpatient psychiatric hospitals offer an opportunity for intensified therapy, monitoring of medications, and time to evaluate the suicidal person's response to both. The programs and environment are geared to returning people to their lives as soon as possible and referring them to outpatient treatment. Due to the high cost of inpatient treatment programs, they are often short term, and are located in or affiliated with a local hospital.

Therapy at an inpatient facility generally involves a treatment team consisting of a psychiatrist, a psychotherapist, and nurses. Most treatment programs include individual and group therapy. Many facilities have special units for adolescents, as well as programs for alcohol and drug abuse, depressive disorders, and eating disorders. Private psychiatric hospitals may offer art therapy, dance and body movement therapy, or recreational therapy.

The price and quality of psychiatric hospitals can vary dramatically. Check out both private and state-run facilities. Private hospitals can be quite expensive. State-run hospitals are much less expensive, but their image can be somewhat negative in the minds of the general public. Don't discount them in your search. There are state hospitals that are as good as private hospitals and many run high quality specialized units (adolescent units or drug and alcohol units, for example). Veterans can receive treatment at any VA hospital on an inpatient and outpatient basis as part of their benefits.

Inpatient psychiatric hospitalization is a major step both emotionally and financially. When deciding whether to hospitalize the suicidal person, consider three things—the lethality of the attempt, how the person feels about not killing himself, and the family's peace of mind. How close did the person come to killing himself? Is he disappointed that he is still alive and still vowing to end his life? Can the family run the risk of not hospitalizing the suicide attempter? How motivated is the suicide attempter to get well?

Hospitalization should not be looked at as frightening or threatening, nor simply as a last resort, but as a chance for the suicidal person to concentrate on getting well and staying well.

Mental Health Professionals—What's in a Title?

Many people are confused by the various titles and credentials used by people in the mental health field. The following is a brief explanation:

Psychiatrist—A psychiatrist is a medical doctor who specializes in the treatment of mental and emotional disorders.

Psychiatrists are the only mental health professionals who can prescribe medication. They've been through four to six years of medical school and one year of internship in general clinical medicine at a hospital. Additionally, a residency of two years of special training in psychology is required for those specializing in child psychiatry; three years is required for adult psychiatrists. Psychiatrists do psychotherapy, either in private practice or with a treatment facility.

Psychologist—The difference between a psychiatrist and a psychologist is that the psychologist cannot prescribe medication and has no medical training. What confuses most people between psychologists and psychiatrists is that psychologists are PhDs and also use the title of doctor. The PhD-level psychologist has gone through three to five years of graduate school in psychology, but no medical school. The clinical psychologist may do psychotherapy and psychological testing (IQ, personality, neurological, etc.). Like the psychiatrist, the psychologist is licensed for private practice and can receive insurance payments. There are masters-level psychologists who carry out the same functions as PhDs, but they are often under the supervision of a PhD-level psychologist or psychiatrist.

Licensed Clinical Social Worker—This person holds a masters degree in social work (LCSW), generally a two-year postgraduate degree. LCSWs may be psychotherapists in private practice or they may work for treatment facilities.

Counselor—This is a term that refers to any of the above-mentioned professionals, or licensed professional counselors (LPC), including marriage and family counselors, and ministerial counselors. If the person refers to himself simply as a counselor, ask what that title means in terms of credentials and training.

Asking the Right Questions

The first question to ask the treatment facility or outpatient therapist is, "How much experience have you had in treating suicidal people?" This is also the most crucial question to ask the outpatient therapist. While almost all psychiatric treatment facilities have had experience with suicidal people, a therapist in private practice may have little or no experience with them. Not all mental health professionals are knowledgeable about the nature of suicide or are comfortable treating people who are suicidal.

Specify the sex and age of the person in question, possibly even his occupation and ethnic background. In cases of young and elderly suicide attempters, it is especially vital that the therapist has worked with those age groups before and has good rapport with them. Not all therapists work well with all people, usually due to the amount of their experience in working with certain populations.

You have every right to ask about the therapist's professional credentials and years of experience. If you are exploring a treatment facility, ask about licensing and accreditation as well as the staff's credentials. Reputable treatment facilities and outpatient therapists welcome these inquiries and will supply you with as much information as you need.

When you've found the therapist or treatment facility that is the most appropriate, ask for a consultation in order to get a firsthand impression. Inquire about fees for the consultation. Outpatient therapists usually charge a fee, while some treatment facilities offer consultation at no charge.

In your consultations, use your instincts. Ask yourself if you feel comfortable with the level of expertise of the mental health professional or treatment facility, and if the treatment program addresses the needs of the suicidal person. Do you feel comfortable with the outpatient therapist as a person, and feel able to talk with him? Do you think the suicidal person can work with him? Does the staff at the treatment facility seem caring and concerned? Will the suicidal person be well-treated here? If the answer to these questions is "No," continue your search.

Successfully Treating the Whole Person

Virtually all suicidal people suffer from clinical depression, which is the result of a chemical imbalance or change in brain activity. The chemicals in the brain that appear to be most involved in depression are called neurotransmitters, which are the chemical messengers that carry signals between brain cells, and which also regulate mood and other brain functions. Clinical depression involves an imbalance in one or more of these messengers. The neurotransmitters serotonin, norepinephrine, and dopamine are most often linked to changes in mood and depression.

Because clinical depression involves a chemical imbalance, the best treatment is a combination of antidepressants, psychotherapy, and possibly changes in diet and exercise. A chemical imbalance cannot be cured simply by talking about it in psychotherapy, nor can a person's difficulties coping with stress be fixed simply by taking a pill.

The first order of business in treating depressed and suicidal people is to have a physician or psychiatrist conduct a thorough evaluation for a physical disorder, for example, an imbalance in the endocrine system. Once a physical problem has been eliminated as the cause, the person should then be evaluated for an antidepressant to correct the imbalance in the brain's neurotransmitters.

Antidepressants

Antidepressants help correct the chemical imbalance or change in brain activity. The most commonly used antidepressants are Selective Serotonin Reuptake Inhibitors (SSRIs), which ease depression by increasing the levels of serotonin in the brain. SSRIs tend to have fewer side effects than other antidepressants.

There are a number of SSRIs, but the most commonly prescribed are Celexa, Lexapro, and Prozac. The doctor or psychiatrist will choose the one they think will work best for each individual.

In general, it takes antidepressants three to four weeks to become most effective. There are possible side effects, but many will go away after the first few weeks. If the depressed person is experiencing side effects that indicate an inability to tolerate a particular SSRI, he may be able to tolerate another one with a different chemical makeup.

Another class of antidepressants, tricyclics, help make the serotonin and norepinephrine that our bodies are already producing more available for use by the brain. Commonly used tricyclics include Elavil and Triavil.

The medications most often prescribed for long term treatment of bipolar disorder are lithium and mood stabilizers. Lithium helps decrease the intensity of the manic (high) episodes and makes the depressive symptoms less severe. Exactly how lithium works is unknown. Mood stabilizers are generally anti-seizure medications.

Antidepressants should always be prescribed with caution and carefully monitored by a psychiatrist or general physician. If a doctor recommends an antidepressant, ask him about side effects and possible complications.

You might want to get a second opinion, especially if the patient is a child, teenager, or elderly person. In the case of children and teenagers, medication should not be used unless absolutely necessary. Psychotherapy, family therapy, improving diet, and exercise are much better ways to treat young people.

Often, the elderly have problems taking antidepressants due to other medications they may already be taking and specific physical problems. If possible, seek treatment or consultation with a psychiatrist, gerontologist, or internist who specializes in working with the elderly.

Psychotherapy

Psychotherapy is the art of helping people see choices and make changes in their lives. It is the process of altering the way a person feels about himself, solves problems, views situations, and deals with life stresses.

The therapist must first find out how the person has tried to work out his difficulties. The therapist helps the suicidal person to understand that there are other ways to deal with problems and then helps him develop the skills to implement these alternative solutions.

There is no "one size fits all" therapy. There are as many forms of therapy as there are therapists. A therapist needs to approach problem solving from a theoretical base (behavioral, cognitive, family systems, Gestalt, Jungian, Freudian, to name a few) yet be flexible enough to allow for the differences in people and their own unique problems. Cognitive behavioral therapy (CBT) is one of the most widely used, and often the most effective, approach to helping someone who is depressed and suicidal.

Psychotherapy for a suicidal person involves changing negative thoughts, feelings, and behaviors. The suicidal person's thoughts and beliefs about himself and the world around him are usually negative and this, in turn, creates negative feelings. These thoughts, beliefs, and feelings are automatic and the suicidal person believes them to be the truth. These attitudes, repetitive feelings, and thought patterns are referred to as low self-esteem or a bad self-image.

The therapist must create a safe, cooperative context in which the person is free to set aside those rigid perspectives and see himself, and the world around him, in a more comfortable and balanced way. It allows the person to be less isolated and more connected to his world, and to develop a more workable future for himself. This is essential in working with those who are chronically suicidal or chronically depressed.

This process can be done in individual therapy with the suicidal person or in conjunction with marital therapy or family therapy, which is often referred to as systems therapy. Systems therapy operates on the belief that "no man is an island"—the suicidal person's relationships with significant others are involved and affected by the suicidal person's behavior and crisis.

Systems therapy treats the relationships between the suicidal person and the significant others. For the suicidal child or young adult, it's very important to get the whole family involved in family therapy, where the emphasis is on improving communications. The goal is better understanding between the suicidal person and significant others. Almost all suicidal people can benefit from both individual and family therapy to arrive at a more permanent resolution of their problems.

Psychotherapy is not magic. The therapist will not be able to fix conflicted relationships or other problematic situations for the suicidal person, but will offer him new ways to do this for himself. The therapist and patient work together through the patient's maze of confusing emotions. Armed with knowledge and skills, the therapist can look at a problem with a fresh perspective and suggest different ways to deal with situations. The suicidal person will hopefully learn new approaches to problems he has been struggling with and develop new coping skills. If a person truly understands that there is another way to approach a situation, he generally feels less depressed.

Nutrition and Exercise

There is a definite link between nutrition, exercise, and depression. Stress appears to affect the way the body digests food. In turn, the way the body digests food affects brain functioning. Researchers are looking closely at the way in which thyroid functioning, hormones, digestive enzymes, and vitamin deficiencies affect depression and other emotional disorders.

Mounting evidence suggests that improper diet or digestive problems can contribute to depression and vice versa. If the body (especially the brain) is not getting the proper nutrients, a person does not feel his best. He cannot handle stress as well and does not think as clearly. It is not unusual for people suffering from depression to eat poorly. Usually, by the time a person is suicidal, his diet is pretty dismal.

After consultation with a nutritionist, many people come to realize that they have been eating improperly for a long time. People under a great deal of stress tend to deal with it by eating more, often the wrong foods, or by not being able to eat at all. Returning to a balanced diet is important in recovering from depression.

In addition, people suffering from depression generally become less active physically. The importance of exercise to mental health is sometimes overlooked, but often the key to getting people unstuck and moving emotionally is to get them moving physically. Physical exercise is a good way to manage stress, relieve anxiety, and enhance functioning. It has been acknowledged that exercise releases endorphins, which are natural antidepressants. Any change in, or addition to, an exercise program should be monitored by a physician.

How Significant Others Can Help the Treatment Process

It is important to continue to look out for the suicidal person after he begins the treatment process. Though he is receiving treatment, he is not yet out of the woods. There are many ways in which you can continue to help while the suicidal person is in therapy. One of the most important is going into therapy with the patient when his therapist feels it is the appropriate time.

Whether you get into the therapy process or not, it is extremely helpful for you to develop a relationship with the therapist. The therapist should be consulted regarding how much responsibility you should take for the suicidal person's daily functioning.

For example, ask whether you should be responsible for making sure the suicidal person takes his medication or doesn't drink alcohol. Should you take over the suicidal person's everyday duties like cooking and cleaning for a while? At what point are you babying the patient? The therapist can give guidance about how to handle the suicidal person, when to encourage him to resume normal activities, and when to back off. You can likewise give the therapist valuable information about the patient's history and how he seems to be coping outside the therapist's office.

You and/or the suicidal person may get frustrated at times. You both may reach a point at which you feel he is not making any progress. Any doubts you may have about his treatment should be discussed with the patient in conjunction with the therapist.

It is highly recommended that you educate yourself and other significant others about what the suicidal person is going through, and what is involved in the treatment process. For instance, you should know about the medication the suicidal person is taking and what the person can and can't eat or drink while on the medication. If kicking a drinking or drug habit is involved in treatment, you can help by keeping an eye on the patient. You must also overcome any stigma you may feel about mental illness. The suicidal person may be quite sensitive about it himself and needs your reassurance.

It is important to continue to be watchful, even when he is in therapy and appears to be improving. The suicidal person's underlying problems may remain, even though his depressive symptoms may be gone and he appears more "up." Discuss any worries you may have with the therapist.

You may find yourself feeling confused, left out, and even resentful about the close relationship between therapist and client. The suicidal person may divulge intimate details of your relationship. Don't be preoccupied with what the suicidal person might be saying. Keep in mind, it's from his point of view and is affected by his emotional reaction to all kinds of past experiences independent of you. Don't push the suicidal person to talk to you about his treatment and problems. He'll open up if he wants to. Above all, don't waste energy feeling guilty about whether or not you contributed to the suicidal person's condition. Concentrate on helping him get better.

As the suicidal person's recovery progresses, it's important to be extra patient with him, but do not deny your own feelings. Perhaps you're getting exhausted and fed up because, despite your efforts, the situation has been going on for a long time. Be honest and discuss your feelings openly, but be careful not to appear as though you're rejecting him. It's okay to say, "We go through these times when you want to kill yourself, and I know you're suffering. Sometimes I get really tired and frustrated, but I care about you and I'm willing to stick in there. I sure hope you are too."

You must be very self-defining in your relationship with the suicidal person. Being overly protective of someone may be damaging in the long run. At this point in the suicidal person's recovery, don't make promises you know you can't keep. In the case of a man who has become suicidal because his wife wants a divorce, the wife would need to be very clear about what she would and wouldn't do for her husband.

Suppose even after marriage counseling, she still wanted a divorce, but was afraid it might cause her husband to kill himself? She couldn't allow herself to get into a bind out of concern for him, rationalizing, "I'll stay with him till he's no longer suicidal, and then leave." She would have to be honest and say, "I care about you. I hope you don't hurt yourself, but I'm not coming back into this relationship. I'll help you in any way I can, short of moving back in with you."

A child may be upset over his parents' impending divorce, or a move to another city. The parents must tell him, "We love you, we'll do anything to help you, but we're still getting a divorce," or "This promotion is very important and means we've got to move. We'll do everything we can to help you adjust and feel better about the change."

The suicidal person may become angry and hurt, but once the situation is clarified, everybody's anxiety level drops. The troubled person's expectations are lowered and he'll stop hoping for the unrealistic goal that the problem will simply undo itself. "I'm clear now, that no matter what I do, she's not coming back to me," or "My parents are still splitting up, and killing myself won't change it."

Be aware that as the suicidal person improves and changes through treatment, your relationship with him will also go through changes. The suicidal person's changes will be positive, but if you are having trouble adjusting, ask the therapist for help.

The Treatment Process

While the treatment process varies, depending on the individual case and philosophy of the therapist, it generally follows the same basic steps for both inpatients and outpatients. The greatest variable is in how long the process takes. In the case of a suicide attempter, his physical condition is treated first. Once he is stabilized and out of danger, the rest of the process ensues. The following story illustrates the treatment process for one suicide attempter.

Suzanne's Story

Suzanne was twenty-five years old when she climbed into a perfumed bubble bath and washed down a few handfuls of pills with expensive champagne. Having been brought up in a well-to-do family, she had decided to go out in style.

Suzanne's mother had gone to a movie, but got there too late. She returned home earlier than expected and found her daughter unconscious in the bathtub. Miraculously, Suzanne's face hadn't slid underwater. Her mother dragged her out of the tub and called 9-1-1. The paramedics rushed Suzanne to the nearest hospital, where her stomach was pumped and her physical condition treated. When she was out of danger and ready to be released, her mother petitioned for involuntary commitment and Suzanne was transferred to a psychiatric hospital.

When she arrived at the psychiatric hospital, her story was taken and her situation evaluated. Like all people who attempt suicide, Suzanne's perception was that her problems were unsolvable. When the hospital staff asked her why she tried to kill herself, she stated that she was a failure. Despite the fact that she graduated Phi Beta Kappa from a prestigious university, was a success in her profession, and extremely attractive, she considered herself inadequate. When asked, "Why?" she gave a long, rambling answer that boiled down to, "I've let my parents down. All their unhappiness is my fault. I'm not perfect." Suzanne was the firstborn child and only daughter. She was the apple of her father's eye—his "little princess"—to be indulged and pampered.

When she was fifteen, Suzanne went to a movie downtown by herself. As she came out of the theater, three men grabbed her and dragged her into an alley. One of them raped her, while the other two held her down. She believed that all three had planned to rape her, until they thought they heard someone coming and fled. Bruised, violated, and in emotional shock, Suzanne was somehow able to pull herself together enough to get home.

Upon hearing what had happened, her mother became hysterical and Suzanne wound up comforting her. Suzanne's father, a prominent local businessman, refused to let Suzanne report the rape to the police. He told her to get in the car. Suzanne thought he was taking her to the doctor. Instead, he drove around for an hour, telling her how ashamed he was of her. Her father felt that if she hadn't been in "that kind of area," the rape wouldn't have occurred. He blamed the victim. Suzanne was so emotionally distraught, that she too began to believe it was all her fault.

The family agreed that the "incident" would never again be mentioned. They never even told Suzanne's younger brothers about it. The family was very successful financially and socially prominent, but not terribly enlightened about certain issues.

Suzanne's mother could not stand up to her husband, but privately told Suzanne that she thought he was wrong and shouldn't have handled things the way he did. She then went on to confide in Suzanne her fears that her husband was seeing another woman.

Suzanne became angry over her parents' response to her plight, but somehow buried her resentment and resumed the roles of good little girl and family princess. Managing to push the rape out of her mind and finish high school, she went on to college, where she had a brief, six-month marriage. Suzanne became depressed when the marriage broke up. She entered therapy, but dropped out after only a few sessions. She grew impatient when the antidepressants her psychiatrist prescribed didn't work instantly, and felt that her psychotherapy sessions were a waste of time.

In the meantime, her parents' marriage broke up and her father suffered serious financial setbacks. Suzanne's mother moved to another town where she had no friends and no emotional support. She called upon Suzanne to move in with her "until she got her life straightened out," consequently shifting her dependency from her husband to her child. Suzanne reluctantly moved in with her. She felt responsible for her mother's happiness and guilty for reasons she couldn't quite pin down. Two months later, she stepped into the bath with champagne and pills in hand, and attempted suicide.

Suzanne had been unable to sleep for several weeks before her suicide attempt. She had lost her appetite, was anxious, irritable, and couldn't think clearly. While she was aware of her confusion, she could not even begin to sort things out.

The staff psychiatrist determined that Suzanne was suffering from a clinical depression and decided the first thing to do was to treat Suzanne's depressive symptoms. The psychiatrist took into account Suzanne's medical history and the antidepressants she had taken in the past, and recommended a course of treatment involving antidepressants, a special diet, individual therapy, group therapy, and an exercise program. She was also placed in an activities program that involved painting and modern dance—two things she'd been interested in before her illness.

Suzanne immediately dismissed the antidepressants saying, "I tried them before, but they don't work for me." It was determined that during Suzanne's previous experience with antidepressants, she was either not given the correct one or had not taken it long enough to give it a chance to work.

People who are desperately seeking help for their pain and despair—particularly perfectionists like Suzanne—look upon antidepressants as the cure-all to give them instant relief. Sometimes they won't even listen when they're told that most antidepressants take from two to three weeks just to begin to take effect and that most likely, the full impact will not be felt for some time after that. Initially, the patient might begin to sleep and eat better. Often, just that will give him some immediate relief, but the genuine effects of an antidepressant are more long-term.

The staff psychiatrist prescribed an antidepressant, and by the end of her first week in the hospital, Suzanne's condition improved somewhat. She was sleeping better, had more energy, and was thinking more clearly. Her anxiety level was down.

By the end of two weeks, Suzanne was oriented to the hospital's routine and ready for more intensive psychotherapy. As Suzanne began to build trust in her therapist and other members of the staff, she was able to talk about the rape. Suzanne and her therapist determined that the roots of her problem were the trauma from the rape, the denial of her anger over her parents' reaction to the rape, her unreal expectations and perfectionism, and her assumption of responsibility for her parents' happiness. Suzanne also experienced deep feelings of shame and believed that she was responsible for the rape.

Suzanne felt a great deal of anger. The most obvious anger was in her disappointment that despite her suicide attempt, she was still alive. She was incensed with her mother for committing her, and hostile with the hospital staff for keeping her there against her will. After she accepted the fact that her mother and the staff refused to simply let her walk out the door, Suzanne demanded that they make her feel better—instantly. In essence, her attitude was, "Okay, since I've got to be here, cure me right now. Make me not hurt like this."

When she was informed that there was no magic wand, Suzanne became even more rebellious and angry. She was a handful for the staff, but they were glad that she was finally expressing the volatile emotions she had buried since the rape. They encouraged her to release her anger and lash out verbally at whomever, whenever she needed.

That confused Suzanne. In the manner in which she was brought up, nice little girls didn't behave that way. The way the staff saw it, behaving like a nice little girl all her life—never expressing anger or asking for her needs to be met— had been detrimental.

In individual and group therapy, Suzanne sorted out the tumult of her inner feelings—her anger with her parents over the way they handled the rape, as well as her anger with herself for not being the "perfect daughter," her sadness over the breakup of her marriage and her parents' marriage, and the feelings of guilt and shame at letting her parents and herself down.

As Suzanne began to think more clearly and listen to new ideas about her attitudes and feelings, she began to see how absurd some of her beliefs were. The staff and other patients challenged her notion that anyone could be perfect. They asked her, "Why would you even want to be perfect? Not being able to make mistakes produces too much anxiety." Suzanne began to see that she was living proof of that.

To tackle Suzanne's unrealistically high expectations of herself, the therapist assigned her to make one harmless mistake every day. One day it might be arriving late to an activities session. Another day, it would be making a misstep in dance therapy. With these little imperfections, Suzanne practiced how to forgive herself for not being infallible.

Suzanne listened to suggestions about how she might deal with things differently, including the way she could deal with her parents. She was at the "Yes, but..." stage. While she agreed in principle that dealing with her parents on a more adult level was a good idea, the thought of actually doing it terrified her.

She was afraid her mother would not be able to handle the "awful" things she had to say. She was particularly afraid that if she told her father how she felt about the way he handled the rape, she would lose what little relationship she had left with him. For some suicidal people, their greatest fear is that they will hurt their significant others if they speak honestly about their feelings. They would, literally, rather die than risk causing pain to the people they love.

The therapist began to give Suzanne ideas about how to tell her parents how she really felt. The therapist coached her in much the same way any other coach works—"Try a different way and see how it feels, see if it works better." When Suzanne became comfortable expressing her feelings to the staff, the therapist decided that the next step would be actual sessions with her father and mother, and eventually, her brothers.

Suzanne met with her mother first. She was nervous and tentative at first, but was able to tell her mother that she felt responsible for her, more like a parent than a child. Suzanne had taken her father's role in her mother's life by giving her emotional support and by being her mother's confidante. Suzanne was tired of being caught between her parents. It had been up to her to let Dad know when Mother needed more money and to make sure he knew how hurt and angry Mother was.

Suzanne's mother responded by saying that she did realize how she had become too dependent upon Suzanne. She talked about her own problems, but began taking responsibility for them. By the end of the third session, Suzanne's mother began to accept full responsibility for her own issues and problems, and released Suzanne from the role of "her mother's keeper."

Due to her parents' conflicted relationship, the sessions with Suzanne's father were separate from those with her mother. This arrangement helped Suzanne to accept her parents' divorce and to learn to deal with her father on her own.

During the first session with her father, Suzanne slouched in her seat and tugged at her sleeve. Her posture became like that of a little girl. At times, her voice would even change and become childlike. Her father would beam at her, calling her his "little princess."

When the therapist asked Suzanne what it was like to be a "little princess," she turned pale and became visibly shaken.

Her father dropped his head and sighed. For the first time in years, he reached out his hand to his trembling daughter and said, "I just want you to know that I love you. I didn't mean to keep you a little girl."

Suzanne looked at her father as though he were a complete stranger and began to cry. Throughout the next four sessions, Suzanne alternated between being a helpless little girl, an outraged teenager, and a self-aware young woman. When she was ready, she confronted her father with the most toxic question of all, "Why did you treat me the way you did when I was raped?" At first her father was defensive, but Suzanne pressed him. She had practiced this question with the therapist over and over.

Eventually, her father apologized, sincerely admitting that he now realized that he had reacted stupidly about the rape. He explained that he was so shocked and devastated that he hadn't wanted to admit that his "beautiful princess" had been raped. Therefore, he forced his denial on the entire family. Suzanne's father said that he now understood the price she had paid for his perfectionism and unreal expectations. Suzanne vented her rage for a few minutes and then cried with relief at being let off the hook after ten years.

The session with Suzanne's brothers consisted of her telling them about the rape. The brothers looked at one another and said, "We knew about that. Mom and Dad thought it was a secret, but just like Dad having a girlfriend, it wasn't much of a secret."

Although the brothers were ten and thirteen at the time of the rape, they'd planned to beat up the men who'd attacked Suzanne and had gone looking for them several times. Suzanne and her brothers laughed at the idea of two kids beating up three big tough guys. At the close of the session, the therapist asked the brothers to tell their mother and father that they had known about the rape all along. Officially, the family secret would no longer be a secret.

Suzanne stayed in the hospital for almost a month and continued to see her therapist as an outpatient for several months after that. Therapy continued to teach her how to deal more constructively with herself and the people she encountered in daily life.

After resigning from the roles her parents had assigned to her over the years, Suzanne went through a confusing period of finding herself. Her mother had moved back to her home town and her old friends. Her father had remarried and Suzanne was maintaining a good relationship with him.

Suzanne successfully resumed her career, remarried, gave birth to a beautiful daughter, and is happy with her life. She says that occasionally the shadow of the past darkens her present world, but when she looks at her daughter, she realizes what she would have missed had she killed herself. She is very clear that it is not always easy to be alive, but it is preferable to the alternative.

The treatment process varies with each individual. The important thing is to find the course of treatment best suited for the individual patient. Researchers are discovering and experimenting with many new kinds of treatments. You must be patient and give it a chance—the person can't get well overnight. Suzanne's story illustrates that suicide is a symptom of underlying emotional problems which can be treated so that the person is no longer suicidal. The suicidal person can be helped to better cope with life and to learn to enjoy living more.

Eight

How Have Others Overcome Suicidal Episodes?

Interviews with People Who Were Suicidal at One Point in Their Lives

This chapter contains eight interviews with people who were once suicidal and have gone on to live productive and, to varying degrees, improved lives. While their stories differ, each person went through a similar process in becoming suicidal. Each suffered personal losses which led to psychological distress and suicidal feelings. Every story has the same message—there are alternatives to suicide. Suicidal feelings and depression are temporary and treatable. Through determination and professional treatment, all of the people interviewed began to see other options.

For several of the people, there was a history of depression and suicidal feelings, and their underlying problems had gone unresolved. Some saw death as an escape from their problems, while others weren't thinking in terms of dying and counted on being rescued in time.

There was also a familial link for several of those interviewed. In one instance, a young man was haunted by a grandfather who had killed himself and his wife years before the young man was born. In another case, the same family stresses contributed to the suicide attempts of both a mother and a teenage daughter. Two other interviewees are brother and sister, but each became suicidal for completely different reasons, long after they moved out on their own.

Some of the people interviewed believed they hadn't given any clues that they were suicidal. It is possible that they unconsciously gave off clues, which significant others failed to pick up on. In some cases, significant others around the person either said nothing, or said the wrong things. As you read these stories, put yourself in the place of the suicidal person's significant others and imagine what you would have said and done in that same situation.

Reading these stories will enable you to understand how it feels to be suicidal, and will, hopefully, inspire you to reach out and try to save a life.

Ken's Story

An estimated 1,600 people have committed suicide by jumping off San Francisco's Golden Gate Bridge. Ken is one of the few who have survived. Ken became suicidal when he felt like he was failing at his job. He survived his first suicide attempt (a pill overdose), but instead of dealing with his depression, Ken tried to forget about it. He returned to graduate school and began a new career in computer graphics, but his mental health problems returned when he began to feel inadequate at his new job. He felt like he'd let his family down after all they had sacrificed to put him through school, and thought that his wife and child would be better off without him. Luckily, he survived the jump, got into therapy, and put his life back together.

How long were you suicidal before you jumped?

I tried once before. In between times, I wasn't suicidal, though.

What were the circumstances?

It was my job. Both times were job-related. I hated myself. I hated my boss. I didn't feel like there was anywhere I could turn to, so I took pills. It didn't work. I woke up an hour later. I took a whole bottle of sleeping pills—they were over-the-counter—and a six-pack of beer. I sat out in my car in a real nice, shady spot and took the pills, drank the beer. I woke up an hour later. I wasn't drunk. I wasn't tired. Nothing. So I drove home. It was weird. Very strange.

Did you tell anybody about it?

I told my wife. And she said, "Well, we won't talk about it." That was the big mistake. We didn't treat it seriously.

You didn't go into psychotherapy?

No. After that, I had counseling for depression, which really didn't help me much. That was later. But we didn't treat it like a serious attempt. I'm not real sure what we were thinking. We were both scared. We didn't want to tell anybody. We didn't want to announce that I was suicidal. So that was really the worst part.

In between the two attempts, I was in pretty good spirits. I went back to school and that helped a lot, because I did very well in school. But after the first attempt, we left it alone and things that led up to my being suicidal again weren't solved.

So, onward and forward. Here, again, it was job-related. I went back to school for two years and I did very well in school. I got out and started working in the real world, and I thought, "This is going to be a breeze."

But here I was, just starting out. Mistakes were not part of my plan. Unfortunately, I did make mistakes. I knew that if I failed this time—because I had failed before—I didn't know how I could face my family. I didn't work while I was in school, so they really had to put up with a lot for two years. I thought, "I can't face them. I can't tell them that I failed after they'd put up with so much." So I just went, "Well, there doesn't seem to be much I can do." I finally decided on suicide. I knew it was a viable solution—*then*, I thought it was. I started thinking, "How can I do it?"

How long were you in a suicidal state before you attempted it?
I'd say three, four days. I was depressed ever since I had the job. When most people start jobs, they will give themselves a grace period, a breaking-in period, right? I didn't even give myself that. I was very harsh on myself.

In those three or four days, were you actively looking for ways to commit suicide?
A day before I jumped, the idea of the jump came to me. The statistics are very good. You're gonna die. And that's what I wanted. I did not want to fail at this. I wanted to die. You're pretty sure you're gonna die. I didn't want it to be messy. I didn't want my daughter or my wife to find me. Nothing messy like a gun or hanging or slitting my wrists or something like that. I said, "I'll just get out of here. I'll leave the world."

Once I finally decided I would do it, deciding how was a little easier. I said, "Hey, the bridge would be great because, maybe they wouldn't find my body. They may never find out where I went."

My biggest worry was that somebody would find me. I wanted to be gone. I wanted to be off the face of the Earth. I wanted people to go forward and I knew they would be better off without me. That was the biggest thing. I really thought I was doing this for them because they'd be better off without me.

After two years in school, I'd failed. I'd only been at my job two months and I was already a failure. This was my thought process before I jumped. Because I knew they'd be better off. I knew somehow they'd get by without me. They'd have a better life. They wouldn't have to worry about me. So I decided to jump, and while I was driving over there, I was really happy.

I'd made a decision, things were within my grasp. I knew what I had to do. I had a goal in life. It was a very short-term goal. I knew that all the pain I'd caused them—all the pain

I'd been feeling—would be over as soon as I jumped.

And you'd be succeeding at something.
Exactly! That was another thing. I felt that I was a failure. But here I am, I failed again (at suicide) and I'm so happy that I failed. It's really kind of funny.

Did you leave a note?
No.

You thought they'd think you'd just disappeared and it would be a great mystery?
Under mysterious circumstances, yeah. The authorities would probably know because my truck was there. And probably somebody would see me jump off. I didn't really think that clearly about it. I was hoping that my body would go in the water and never come back up.

I was very happy about what I was going to do because I knew the pain was going to be over. I finally got to the bridge and I looked at it and it was very formidable. It's huge. It's a long way down. I had second thoughts when I went into the parking lot. I said, "I'm going to be very strong about this. I've got to do this. I can't be swayed by—that it might hurt or something like that. I've got to be strong."

I knew that this was the best thing for everybody. That's what kept me going. I got out on the bridge and I was really, really scared because I didn't know what would happen after I died. I've never been afraid of death. I'm still not afraid of death. But I was looking it in the face and it really kind of shook me up a little bit.

While I was at the railing, it took me quite a bit to finally jump. I really had to dig deep to finally say, "I've got to do it. If not for myself, for everybody else." I counted to ten... I didn't jump. I counted to ten again. I didn't jump. I counted to ten the third time, put my hands on the railing and vaulted over. That's when all hell broke loose.

I was terrified. Once I finally realized what I had done and where I was going and all the things that I was missing, I was terrified. Remorse is really a light word compared to what I felt at that time. From the time that I left the bridge to the time I blacked out—because I blacked out on the way down, I would say a quarter of the way down—every emotion, every bad emotion that I could feel, I felt.

It was so terrifying, so horrible, so sad. Because I'd wasted everything. You know, for twenty-eight years, I'd wasted it. I'd done nothing. Destiny brought me to the bridge to die and that was it. I felt really sad that that's all I could have done.

You immediately regretted it and wanted another chance?
Yes. If I could have jumped back on the bridge and stood there again, I would have left and gotten help. I'd have gone to the doctor right away. I still wish I could have.

Again, here it was, I knew what I had to do. I had this goal. I knew it was the right thing to do. And all of a sudden, it turns around. If there's any way to immediately, within microseconds, completely, turn around 180 degrees, that's what I did. It was so quick. It was just incredible that I wanted to live so bad. And maybe this is what saved me.

I hit the water. I had to have been swimming unconsciously, because when I woke up I was already swimming. When I was still in the water, I was terrified. I was saying, "Oh God, help me out of this. I need some help." I really didn't know if I was going to live. But now I wanted to. I blacked out again, and then I was on the Coast Guard cutter.

The moment I got on the cutter, I knew I was going to live. The doctors didn't know if I was going to live. I had a couple of broken ribs and one lung was bruised, but it didn't collapse. That was about it. My butt was real bruised up, because that's how I landed, you know, a cannonball.

The irony was, now you wanted to live.
In those few seconds of falling, I decided to live, instead of fighting to die. And it was just incredible. They took me to the hospital and I was in intensive care for a day and a half. I got out of intensive care and got out of the hospital in five days, and I was back home. That was it.

Did you seek therapy?
Oh yeah. They said, "Before we can let you out of the

hospital, we have to have verification that you're going to a therapist immediately after discharge." And I said, "Hey, listen, don't you ever worry about me getting therapy, because I'm going whether you guys want me to or not. I'm going to therapy because I'm in trouble." I was smart enough to realize that I had a dangerous tendency, a danger towards myself. And that if I didn't get it resolved, maybe next time I would succeed. I didn't want to do that. I didn't want to ever feel that again.

You were an outpatient? No psychiatric hospital?
No. I went once a month. My wife and I went.

Did they put you on antidepressants?
No.

Did therapy also help your marriage?
Oh, yeah. We're really a lot stronger now, because I stick up for myself. It creates tension which then increases activity and instead of, "Oh yeah, dear, go ahead and do it, whatever you want to do," I'll say, "No, forget it." She puts up with it because she realizes the alternative of my not talking. I go inward and things start boiling over.

How would you describe yourself before the attempt?
Neurotic. Very low self-esteem. My self-esteem is a little bit better. I still worry that people don't like me. I still worry that my boss is going to fire me, for no real reason. But I'm working on it. It's a slow process. I try not to worry about things like that, because I do my best and whether people like it or not, it's as much work as I can give. I feel sorry for the person I was before. I still have low self-esteem. It doesn't turn around in a day. It helps me to put in perspective some of the things that I thought were important. I feel that I am good at some things. I give myself credit more often than I used to.

Would you describe yourself as a perfectionist?
Yeah. No question. But I don't work at it that hard. I sit there and I go, "I tell you, I should have done this better, I should have done that better," but I'm not a "Type A" person. I

don't sit and work twelve hours a day. I put in eight hours. But in the eight hours, I worry is it good enough for them? Is that what they want? And that's when it really gets into trouble.

With your second attempt, did you think about your first attempt?

I didn't. It didn't register. It never did come to the forefront, "Hey, you've done it once before. It scared you then. You better think about this again." Nah. I was in a sorry, sorry state. I was so down on myself, and so wanted to help my family that it never did come to the forefront of my thoughts. I knew that I was depressed. I knew I needed professional help, but I didn't have the guts to ask for it and that's the biggest problem. That I didn't say, "Hey, don't be a wuss. Go do it." I felt people would not take me seriously if I said I was suicidal. I really believed that.

Were you embarrassed about asking for help?

Yeah. I didn't want people to say, "What a chump." Here's another story altogether. Two years before, just before I went back to school, I ran away from my job and my family and everything. Caught a bus here in town and went to Chicago. I backed off from everything that I knew. I called my wife two days later and said, "Can I come back?" My wife's put up with a lot in the last eight years.

The biggest problem was about three months after the jump. After the shock had worn off and we were back to the normal grind, she started feeling like she didn't want to be around anymore. She really thought seriously about leaving me. The best thing that happened during the therapy (was that) they said, "Communicate." We talked about how she felt, and eventually she grew to understand what she was feeling and stayed.

Do you think you gave off signals either time?

No, neither time. I was the perfect neighbor, perfect husband, perfect father. I was very good at acting like everything was normal. That's what almost killed me. Nobody could tell.

What would you have wanted people to do for you?

I wish that somebody would have said, "What the hell are you doing?" Had come out to me, straightforward, and said, "What is wrong with you?"

If somebody had asked if you were suicidal, you would have told him?
Yeah. I wouldn't lie to people. If somebody would have asked me, "Are you suicidal?" I wouldn't have lied to them. I would have said—well, this is why I had that whole thing, so that nobody would ask me. I had this beautiful facade that I put up so that nobody would ask me. Nobody knew that I was depressed or unhappy or anything like that. Like I said, if somebody had asked me, I wouldn't have lied... well, maybe I would have. I don't know. I really don't. I didn't want people to know I was suicidal because I thought somebody would stop me.

What would you suggest to people who know a suicidal person? How should they handle it?
You've got to communicate no matter what happens. Just talking about it will not solve all the problems, but it really brings into perspective what the problems mean as opposed to dying. What we're talking about is not living, not being around for that other person. You are depriving him of you. If a person is always talking about suicide, he needs professional help. He needs to get to a psychologist, a psychiatrist. I had a licensed social worker. He was fine, he was really good. The thing is, the suicidal person's mind goes nuts. Relationships and everything are skewed. Everything is sort of looked at from kind of a different angle. And the more I thought about things, the more skewed it got. The more weird it got.

Can you think of an example?
If I'd thought realistically, I would have known that with my suicide, there would have been grief, there would have been horror, it would have torn my family apart. I would have realized that they wouldn't just go on with their lives. I figured that they would have looked for me, they wouldn't find me, my wife goes back to work, and everything's jolly because this ten pound weight is taken from around all of their necks.

This is how I thought it would be. I figured they would just go on with their lives, happy as could be from day one. No remorse. I didn't think there would be grief. I didn't think they'd worry about it. Their lives would be happier because I wasn't in them. They'd be so relieved to get rid of me. This is what my thinking was. I can sort of manipulate the information that's going into my brain so that it sounds even worse.

Anything that I think is geared that way, so every input I get shows that I'm right, because I have to be right. Because if I'm wrong, then something's wrong. Everything is internalized. You get no outward feedback. Does that make sense? It's all internalized. Therefore, you can manipulate the data any way you want and it comes out right, because nobody's there to say it's wrong. You always rationalize it, and it sounds so logical. Like what I just said. It's so illogical that they would go on with their lives the next day, but it sounded very logical to me at the time.

Did you see everything negatively?

No, not really. I thought that it was me. I thought the world was very good, except for me. I was that cancerous growth that needed to be excised. I was the problem. And I could provide my own cure. This would make life better for everybody. I don't feel like that anymore, though. Life's jolly now. It's tough sometimes. It's very, very tough, but I never think of suicide again. Never. I go day by day. I don't think, "Well, I made it through another day. Wow. I'm so happy that I'm living again." I'll go day by day not being suicidal, not thinking suicidal thoughts. I've gone through tough times at work where I thought I was going to get fired. Things haven't gone right. And I've survived them. I'm very proud of myself that I've survived.

You know, to other people, it really wouldn't be that big a deal. You have tough times at work all the time. But to me, it's a major event to get through these things because of how I reacted last time. But will I ever think suicidal thoughts again? I sure hope not. I don't think so. But it's happened, and it could happen again. That's scary. That's one of the reasons why I talk about it. Because it keeps it real. It keeps it up to date. It's not something that happened a long, long time ago.

You like yourself better now?
I do. No matter what I do or how I feel, I have worth to several people.

How does your family react to the new you?
Fine. They don't react much differently because my personality has really not changed a whole lot. So I'm a pretty happy guy. Maybe I'm a little more outspoken, but they don't mind. They haven't reacted negatively at all. At first, sure. Everybody was saying, "Why? Why? Why did you do that? What could I have done?" More my wife, because she sees me day after day. Even my brothers, and sometimes I don't see them for months on end. That's a real normal reaction. It settled down to a very nice relationship. I'm a little more... I speak my mind a little bit more, but it helps immensely.

Can you think of something that you wish they'd done for you?
I really believe talking about the problem alleviates the problem. Communication saved my life. It's so tough, but talking to my wife, saying to her, "I'm going to get fired," and she says, "Okay, so what? You'll get another job. Being fired means nothing, compared to having you still around." If you communicate, you start bringing perspective that the suicidal person does not have. Because, if he internalizes it, he doesn't have any perspective. He can skew it any way, but if you bring in outside information, it makes the person think.

What's the most important thing you learned from this experience?
I'm feeling good again because I can see other options. Suicide is no longer a viable option. And until it becomes an obsolete option, the suicidal person will always think about it. That's the problem—if it's a viable option, you're stuck. The person thinks about it. If you can make it so that it's the worst option available, then the person can get healthy and well.

Dorothy and April

Dorothy and April are a mother and daughter who became suicidal—April first, then her mother, a year or so later. For fourteen years, the family centered around the youngest daughter, who has a severe intellectual development disability (IDD), which experts said would never improve. Their problems can be traced to the pressures and guilt over her condition.

The mother, Dorothy, felt guilty over bringing a disabled child into the world and wanting a life of her own, but suppressed her anger and depression. When she finally placed her child in an institution, her suicidal crisis occurred because of guilt over the relief she felt. Dorothy spent time at a psychiatric hospital and in therapy. Having rebuilt her life, she finally feels she's becoming her own person. Her marriage has improved, and she and her husband are enjoying their newfound opportunity to travel. A contributing factor to her recovery is that her child is flourishing at the institution.

Dorothy's middle daughter, April, felt guilty about asking for any attention from her parents (common among siblings of ill or disabled children) and over having an extremely high IQ. She grew up with low self-esteem and confused self-worth. Forced to take adult responsibilities for the care of her sister and the emotional functioning of the family, April acted out the depression her mother had at first denied. She first considered suicide in sixth grade, and attempted to kill herself when she was seventeen. Through therapy, April went from being withdrawn to outgoing and vivacious. She has become engaged and was just about to leave for a career in the armed forces when interviewed. April is anxious to get on with her life and not look back—which is common among teens who have attempted suicide.

April's Story

What do you remember about your suicide attempt?
I took an overdose of Valium in my bedroom. It was September. It was football season. I don't remember a lot of the things that they told me had happened. I guess I passed

out, because I was so sleepy all of a sudden. I'd never taken Valium before. We were in the car and I remember waking up and my boyfriend telling my father not to drive so fast because he was going to kill me.

What led you to that point?
I thought that no one loved me. No one cared. No one paid enough attention to my problems. I thought that, seeing as how they were my problems, suicide was the solution to it. That was how I could take care of it because there was no other way. No one was gonna help me with it. It never occurred to me to ask.

You never did ask?
I don't know. It's like I hadn't tried hard enough to ask, because I thought people wouldn't pay any attention or think I was crazy or something.

How old were you when you did this?
I'm nineteen now. I guess I was seventeen. Junior year.

How did your parents react?
I think they were shocked. They didn't know how to handle it. I know this is going to sound crazy, but it offended them. It's like they're older and it disrupted their lives. They were really surprised. I remember my father coming in my room and telling me that, no matter how much it would cost, he would make me better. He didn't care about anything else.

What did that mean to you, him saying that?
Well, I didn't expect it. It's like, he was always there, but he was quiet. It made me realize that I wasn't all by myself. I didn't have to go through it alone. He loved me. He did.

How did your mother react?
I don't really remember. I guess it's because in situations like that, my father handles them. My mother is in the background. I know she was always there supporting me lovingly, but I don't remember much about her. My older sister, Lori, surprised me the most. You know, she's my sister, but we never

told each other that we loved each other. She was crying and that just shocked me, because I could not understand after fifteen years of telling each other how ugly we were, that she would cry. But she did.

What is the major reason you attempted suicide?
I was lonesome. I didn't have anybody to talk to. I didn't— I don't know, I was just feeling bad. Most of the time, I couldn't talk without crying. I couldn't say anything without starting to cry. I have no idea why. I was real emotional and real hateful.

Did you tell anyone that you were thinking of killing yourself?
No.

Did any of your friends try to find out what was wrong?
I didn't have any friends that were that close. The ones who did try to find out, it was like I was a teenager, I was depressed, all teenagers get depressed. That's part of growing up, of being a teenager. So that doesn't matter. They just didn't realize the depth of it. Somehow they didn't try.

If you'd had a friend who had the guts to call your parents and say, "Hey, I'm really worried about April," how would you have felt?
I probably would have gotten better immediately. [laughs] I was scared to death of my parents! I guess I would have talked to them. But my family and I didn't talk. Before I went through therapy, we really didn't talk to each other. We'd talk about the weather or about television programs. We'd talk about how my younger sister was doing or how I was doing in school. But that's it.

We never even talked regarding my therapy. It was like, "We've got to go see the therapist next Tuesday," and that was all that was said. Until the therapist told us to sit down for five minutes and talk about ourselves. That was the worst night of my life. I was just sitting there, thinking, "Oh hell. I hate this!" My mother and father hated it too. "We're never going to go see her again. We're going to another psychiatrist who doesn't make us do things like this." But, it helped.

Why do you think you never talked to one another?
I don't know. I think it stems from my mother, because my mother is afraid of confrontations. She talks to me now. My mother and I will sit up late sometimes. And my father—he's just really quiet, the strong silent type.

What was it like for you when your mother took the gun and went down into the basement?
Scared me to death. I didn't know what to do. I was laying on my bed and it was so weird because all of a sudden, something told me, "Go check on your mother." And I went, "What?" because I was half asleep. "Get up and go check on your mother." So I got up and she was heading downstairs with a gun. I thought, "My God, she's gonna die." I got my father. And I cried a lot.

I sat up all night long. My father and my mother were in the living room, so I was in my room. I went into the living room and they were sitting at opposite ends, smoking cigarettes. They weren't even looking at each other. When my mother left for the hospital it was, like, "What if she never comes home? What if she stays in there the rest of her life? At least she'd be alive." Then she got better and I was so happy.

For months after that, I walked around on eggshells trying not to upset her. I still do that when she gets mad and won't talk to me. I didn't have any money on Father's Day, and had to wait until the day after to buy my father a present. My mother got mad because I didn't have a present for him on Father's Day. I couldn't believe her.

What did you get out of the family therapy sessions?
I realized why my mother does it. She's afraid of confrontation. It's the worst thing in the world for somebody to be mad at her, so she's mad at them first. But she doesn't know what to say when she gets mad at them, so she just doesn't talk to them.

You think you're better dealing with anger than she is?
Yes, because I'll yell, I'll scream, I'll stomp my feet.

Were you thinking in terms of killing yourself?
No.

In what kinds of terms were you thinking?
Getting away. Getting out of it. Anything would have been better. Maybe somewhere down in my mind I was thinking that maybe I wouldn't die. That somebody would find me and take me and help me. But I wasn't really thinking about dying.

When you look back at that, how do you feel?
I'm glad I didn't succeed in killing myself. Because it's not so bad. I'm going to get married. I met this wonderful man who loves me, even when I'm not good. He loves me when I'm bad. Without any reservations. I just can't believe that! It's like, I'm a bitch, and he's, "I don't care. I love you anyway."

Wonderful. When are you getting married?
Probably after about a year. He wants to get married right now. He was born and raised to get married and have kids, but I wasn't. I'm having a wonderful time. I know I would have nothing if I'd killed myself. I'm so glad I didn't. Because it's so wonderful to be free. It's like, there's something that's not here anymore, something that didn't belong.

Can you describe that "something?"
Yeah, it was like something was in my rib cage, holding me down. It kind of hurt. Part of the time, I felt there was this big ball in my stomach, with iron spikes on it. You know how you feel when you're really disappointed? It's like, "Uhhhh." It sort of felt like that in my heart all the time. It doesn't feel like that anymore.

How long had you felt that way before you tried suicide?
Since I was in sixth grade. I felt that I had no self-worth. I didn't think anyone liked me. Of course, it was true, no one did like me in sixth grade. I remember coming home one evening and pouring Lysol and Ajax in a glass and I was going to drink it. I smelled it and threw up. I didn't try to kill myself then. I just went back to school.

I used to have a speech problem I was unconscious of. I did it all the time, and people made fun of that. I hated that. I don't know if I hated them doing that or I hated to be noticed. Because I just wanted to live in obscurity, have nobody notice me. It wasn't like they made fun of it all the time. It was like once, for two weeks, and then they found somebody else to pick on. That was the first time I remember feeling bad. I had this best friend who didn't want me to live an anonymous life. I don't know whether I want to thank her or choke her.

You mean, she wouldn't let you disappear into the woodwork?
Uh-huh. I'd come to school with my head down, walk around watching people's feet, never looking at anyone. I never smiled. Never made anybody's day brighter, never made it any worse. She kind of got the message across that I was too pretty to do this. I was fat, I was ugly, but she saw that I was gonna be pretty. So she picked me up and threw me out into people. It worked for a while. Then I found ways to get around her, which was a really dumb thing to do. She was really great and if I ever become a millionaire, I'm going to give her half of it.

Were you afraid of people not liking you?
Yeah. So, I didn't like them. Didn't interact. I was me, in my world. Go away. Things are different now. At work, my last day, people gave me these little notes they'd written to me. Things like, "Wonderful" and "Vivacious" and I'm just going, [laughs] "No, you've got me confused. Not me."

So that's the difference between now and a couple of years ago?
I think I've sort of grown into being who I am. It's like, when I was suicidal, I had reached the break-off point. It's like here I was, and I could either go down or go up. I wanted up.

What would you say to other kids about feeling suicidal?
That it's not worth it. No matter how bad it looks, it's gotta get better. Because there's nowhere else you can go.

There's no farther down that you can go. It's really not worth it, because when you come back, it's great. I tell people what I think, but people who are depressed won't listen to a word I say.

People like that, it's like they have this wall, this curtain around them that just backs everyone off. Somehow, you've got to get under that. You don't get through it, you get under it. It's a lot easier that way. It's like, "Why don't you come out with me? We can go to town and hang out." That works. Then, it's not like you're talking down to them. You're on neutral ground, and you can say what you want to and they're not intimidated. It's a lot simpler that way.

What else have you learned going through this?
That people aren't out to get me. They aren't out just to make me miserable. And people like me better if I'm not laying on the floor, waiting to be kicked. If I talk to people, they're going to talk to me. I used to have the attitude, "You don't like me and I don't like you, but it's better because I don't like you first." I mean, that's awful.

I've got so many friends now, since I got a job and got over being what I was. It's so nice. I see people who don't like other people because they're afraid that they don't like them. So I'm friends with them, and if they don't like me, that's not my problem.

People are going to like you, but you've got to put forth the effort. They're not going to like you because you're just sitting here like a lump. Now people come to me for advice, and I'll say, "What?" I don't know what to tell them. We talk and then they say, "You should be a psychiatrist," and I say, "You should have your head examined."

How do you feel about leaving to join the service?
I'm dreading it and I'm looking forward to it. I wish I'd never met my boyfriend now, because I'm going to have to leave him. But I want to go and be someone and do something. I can't wait to start my life. About a year ago, I started thinking about this, and people would look at me and say, "You're joining the service? Little, bitty April?" I may be little, but I can do it, I hope. I know I can. It's gonna be hard, but that's

part of the reason I'm doing it. I've had it so easy all my life. I don't think I'll be spoiled anymore, though.

Dorothy's Story

How did you get to the point of feeling suicidal?
There was no hope. Tomorrow was just going to be as bad as today was. There was no light at the end of the tunnel, you could say. It wasn't going to get any better because my youngest daughter was intellectually developmentally disabled, and she was going to be this way for the rest of her life. This is horrible, but I was stuck with her. If I did anything about it (like put my daughter in a home), all these people are going to think I'm a really horrible person, and I'm going to have failed because I couldn't take care of her. I didn't know what else I was going to do. There was no hope.

So one day, I went down to the basement with a gun. My husband heard me—I wanted him to hear me. I really and truly wanted him to hear me. I said to my daughter the other night, "Why was it necessary for me to go to these lengths before I got some help?" She said, "Daddy's just the kind of person you have to kick in the teeth before he really will understand." So I guess that's it. But I did get the attention. I most certainly did.

Then you went into the hospital voluntarily?
Right. The very next day. I wanted to go because I felt so guilty. I wanted to get out of the house, because I couldn't stand it anymore. I had to get out of there and get some help. I didn't really want to die, but I couldn't stand myself anymore.

You wanted out of the situation, but you didn't want to die?
Right. But I believe I could have been pushed into it, if it had gone on. I don't know. If the guilt had just kept building up inside me the way it was.

Were your other daughters affected by all this?
Yes.

April became depressed herself and made a suicide attempt?
Yes, but the thing that really bothered me was that she just disappeared for three days before. I knew the attempt wasn't going to kill her. I knew it wasn't the real thing. It was a cry for help, a need for attention. It was for us to do something to help her.

And your other daughter, Lori, finally said, "To heck with this," and got married?
She got married. Of course, there was a big empty space there, because she eloped. In the spring, I was so bad off. That is when we admitted my youngest daughter to the center. That was a bad year, but it was almost a year before it got worse. A lot of my problems were tied up in being a mother. Mother's Day came. Burt, my husband, did not buy me a Mother's Day present. April did not buy me a Mother's Day present. And that was it. "You are a horrible failure. They realized that you are really a rotten person. And they're not pretending anymore. They really know what you are now." And I couldn't take that. That was it.

If Mother's Day came up now and they didn't...
I'd say, "Why in the hell didn't you buy me something?" Not exactly to that effect, but I would not be crushed.

What was it like being in a psychiatric hospital?
I was terribly intimidated. Scared absolutely to death, although I had visited over there when my sister was hospitalized. I hadn't seen anything strange, but I was only there for a very short time. But my desire to go was so great, that I was going to face that rather than stay home.

I was really concerned that they not think that I was crazy. "What are you doing here?" "Oh, I'm just a little depressed. I'm not crazy!" I had a room to myself, which was really great, because growing up in an alcoholic home, with several sisters and a brother, you really value your privacy.

It was hard for me to reach out to the other people there but they kind of cornered me. They just included me and when I tried to get away from them, they'd come and get me. You know, "Eat with me." They had group therapy with me. I couldn't get away from them.

Psychodrama was interesting. Everybody is in a circle, and since I was so intimidated and basically really shy and insecure, the hardest part of it, for me, was when it came my turn to tell how the last couple of days (before the suicide attempt) had been. I was going to have to talk, and I couldn't talk. I saw people bring out things that had caused them so much pain, real terror. You could feel it, you could see the emotion in the people. They did get a lot out of that.

I didn't want to do psychodrama, but it's like, "If you want to go home, you're going to do psychodrama." So I did psychodrama and mine was the day that we applied to the home for my youngest daughter—how difficult it was and the hard time it was applying for her. I don't know why it was so hard.

At the time, I didn't want to do that to my child. And I couldn't bring it up to the surface. Just couldn't face it. That was being a bad mother. A bad person. A bad human being. A bad wife. But there at the last, I wasn't a very nice person anyway. I couldn't really communicate with anybody. I was just kind of existing.

You were pretty much withdrawn?

Oh, yeah. I started isolating myself when I was a child to get out of the house, away from the drunken quarrels that were happening. I started that at an early age and then I just continued it. I tried to continue it at the hospital. They wouldn't let me.

What do you think you got from hospitalization?

I didn't gain anything until I got out of the hospital, because I was still intimidated while I was over there. Very, very intimidated. It was starting outpatient therapy when I could really think and explore some of the things I had been told over there. It's like when they told me that I had choices, I didn't really believe it at the time. I only learned later you really do have choices. No matter what, you do. They also told me, "You can take a risk." I didn't know till later that you can take a risk. You can and you can live, and you can benefit from it. I'm glad I went over there and got out of the house for a while. I got away from my family and had a chance to be with other people.

How do you feel about having been in a psychiatric hospital?

Now that I have been there and know that there's nothing horrible and scary — maybe sometimes it was a little scary for me — but it doesn't touch me. Education does marvels for you. As you become better educated about a thing, you know more about it, you feel more comfortable about it.

How long were you there?

Nine weeks.

How long were you in outpatient therapy?

About a year. The most important thing my therapist said was, "Don't think of yourself as being sick." That is what stood out in my mind. I'm so thankful she said that to me.

Was guilt the major thing you were dealing with?

Yes, definitely the guilt.

How did you manage to resolve that?

Someone said to me, "Imagine yourself in a room full of people who are very, very intelligent. They are so smart that you have nothing in common with them. In fact, you can't even carry on a conversation with them." Then it hit me that my daughter is like that.

She can't relate to me, really. She can't carry on a conversation with me. She does not perceive things the same way I perceive them. She has a life of her own. I'm not her be-all world. She is entitled to a life of her own where she can be the happiest. She has more freedom where she is now than she ever had with the four of us looking after her. We didn't even go to the bathroom without telling each other, "You look after her, I'm going to the bathroom." It was just a habit we picked up because we just did not leave her alone.

Your entire family was organized around her?
We had to be. I don't want to live like that ever again.

And you do have a choice?
Yes, I do. She is over there because it is my choice for her to be there. That's so hard to say. You couldn't choke that out of me a year ago.

There's always been three of me. One of them has been the lady in charge, doing everything. The other is the lady with the poker up her ass. The third one is the little girl who's like a puppy who's going to wag her tail so she gets her way and you won't be mad at her. I'm trying to get rid of all of those and just be myself.

One of the main ways is with my husband. When I did something I thought he didn't like, I was like a little puppy wagging its tail, "It's okay. I'm not dangerous. I'm not bad. You'll love this once you get used to it." I'm not going to do that anymore, and that's caused some problems between us because (now) I make my own choices and I'm not really worried, "Hey you're not going to like this. You won't like me anymore if I'm being me." I say what I mean. And when something bad happens, I don't rush to placate him like his mother would do, or comfort and console him and say, "Calm down, it's going to be okay."

We've had a few sharp words several times. When I would placate him, he would be so much sweeter and nicer and loving. I'm not as nice as I used to be in that way. But I'm more me and I feel better when I'm me than when I'm phony. I don't do what I don't want to do anymore.

How did playing the three other people fit into getting to the point where you were taking the gun into the basement?
Because I wasn't me. The lady in charge wasn't really in charge. The lady in the middle wasn't really that strong. She just wanted to give that impression. That little girl has to grow up and be a woman and mother, and hopefully, a grandmother. You can't be a little girl and be a grandmother too. You have to grow up.

I'm still learning. I've not cast them all aside at once, just like that. After all, life is a learning process. It goes on from day to day. Tomorrow, you learn something else. It's not like graduating from law school, "Well, I'm through with this, through with learning." That doesn't happen.

How is it—feeling like yourself?

You can be just you. You don't have to pretend to be something you're not. You don't have to give sermons on what it means to be a good mother—"A good mother should do this, a good mother should do that." A good mother should do what feels right for her and what she feels is right for her child. I am a good mother because I put my daughter in a place where she can have more freedom. I am better off. The whole family's better off because of that. It feels good to be an adult. When you act like a child, you're treated like a child. I do want to be an adult.

I still tend to isolate myself, but I'm more free with people than I used to be. I talk more. Now I stand by my convictions against any argument that my husband brings to me. I can do it. Before, I would have caved in, "Well, you're right." No more.

When one person in a family system changes, it affects everyone. How's your husband adjusting to the differences in you?

He loves the fact that I make decisions now and he doesn't have to make all the decisions. But a couple of months ago I made one, and he wasn't overjoyed with it. And I felt so guilty because he wasn't overjoyed. I got so ill and so hateful there for a few days. The guy didn't know what was going on. It was because I was feeling guilty because he was not overjoyed about my decision to do this. Then I told myself, "He doesn't have to be overjoyed about every one of your decisions. Next time, sit down—sincerely —and talk about something before you make a decision, then you won't be left feeling like this."

You can survive standing up for yourself. The family can survive.

Yes, they can. They don't have to protect me any longer. But they will because it's a way of life with them. They will until I put a stop to it. Sometimes it's easier not to make any decision. To just let it ride. Don't take the risk.

How are things today?
I feel good. I went to school for about three months this past spring. Enjoyed it immensely. I spoke out in class. Probably will take something else this fall. Probably psychology again, because I liked it so much. What if I fail? What would happen? Nothing. The world is not going to come to an end. Nobody's looking at you. Unless you fall and bust your ass—they might laugh a couple of minutes. But the world is not really paying that much attention to you. Unfortunately, for your ego.

How do you feel about your life in general at this point?
Better about it. Happier. I got scared for a while. I thought I was becoming one of those mentally ill people because I feel happy all of a sudden. Just like smiling, and like, "Hey, everything's okay." I thought, "Am I becoming ill? Is there something wrong?" I realized it's just because all the stress and all the guilt is taken away. I'm free to be happy. I don't have to feel guilty anymore. It's great.

Ellen's Story

Ellen was abandoned as an infant and spent her first two years in an orphanage until her mother got married and reclaimed her. When she was in her mid-twenties, she began to feel suicidal after experiencing a series of devastating losses which probably triggered early childhood feelings of abandonment—her first husband's death from cancer, her own bout with cancer, bankruptcy, and a divorce from her second husband.

All the while, she was undergoing a crisis of faith. The strict Christian fundamentalist religion in which she was raised was no longer working for her. She neglected seeking professional psychotherapy for years because the doctrines of the church forbade it. She was very depressed, but received little emotional support from significant others. Eventually, psychotherapy helped Ellen out of her depression. She went on to a high-pressure, very profitable career in sales, and a good relationship with another man.

Give a brief description of how you became suicidal.

Well, my first husband died of cancer. I had no one to talk to. My parents were really nice, but... I just started feeling like no matter what I did, I couldn't get by. I'd been through his long illness and subsequent death. I wasn't trained for any kind of work, but as soon as my husband died, I was supposed to be a full, working, participating member of society. It was just too much. I could barely get a job that kept enough money coming in, I was being harassed because of debts for the next couple of years, and it just went on and on.

In the fundamentalist religious group I was in, you weren't allowed to get therapy. I even asked. They told me I should just talk to people in the church and that should help. They didn't hold a gun on me, but their advice was that regular therapy was of the devil. So unbelievable!

For the first year, I was sort of okay. I don't remember very much. I was sort of wacky, but I wasn't dealing with all this death stuff. The next March, I got a tumor that put me in the hospital. I said, "All I want is for people to tell me they love me and bring me flowers."

I was so out of it at the time. The church was no longer working. I had to take a job working for a man who is one of the most horrible people in the world, consequently there was a lot of pressure working for him. Anyway, that was it. I just stopped being the person that I was, but I had no idea who I was. I went around for a long time having never learned that I was okay inside. Which is why I left the church to begin with.

How did you feel?

I told my therapist that I felt like I was standing in a room with a hundred doors and no matter what door I opened, I should have opened a different one. I couldn't figure out if there was any reason to go on. I never would say, "I want to die." I was God-fearing Christian then. It wasn't until I spent time with my second husband and had gotten more out into the world that the idea of suicide and dying became an option.

We had this great year or so. And then, everything began to come up. I began reading feminist literature. I was so angry! I turned thirty. I was in and out (of feeling suicidal) but it was pretty acute at the time my husband and I separated, and then just after I met my present boyfriend it just sort of reared up again, and then it was done. I don't even remember the whole time frame.

Did you finally seek therapy?
I went to therapy after the tumor.

Do you think you gave off signals that you were suicidal?
I said to my second husband, "Look, I think I'm a really nice person and I can do a lot of really neat things, but nothing counts enough. There's just nothing happening. It isn't worth this. I'm always sad. Nothing feels really good. I'm totally miserable. It just isn't enough. I'm not enough—no matter what I do, I should have been doing something else. Somebody's always disappointed." Even in therapy, there came a place where I used to say that I wanted out. I didn't want to do it anymore.

I started asking people, "Why do you live?" and they'd give me these stupid answers, "Well, I'm curious." People who'd never really thought about it. Or they'd go, "I don't know."

I was looking for someone to tell me why they were living—what made it worth it to them—so that I could figure out what made it worth it to me. It was only through eons of therapy that I began to understand that I couldn't adopt anyone else's reason for being here.

I think what happened is that I finally decided, "Either I have to get out of life, or I have to go on with life." I must have been in that place where I actively wanted to die for about two years. I think the reason I stayed alive was that everybody's answers were so ridiculous, I couldn't believe it.

The last time I thought about suicide was when I met my present boyfriend—that's been three years. I came up against something with him—I don't remember what it was—and I said to him, "Wow, I just can't stand this anymore." I left the room and wrote notes to every person I knew, saying just what I wanted. I showed them to my therapist and she said to me, "This is not a person speaking out of anger. This is a person speaking out of sadness. This is a place where somebody doesn't really understand how to make it not hurt like that."

Did you make a plan or attempt?

I talked to my brother several times about how I would kill myself, because I only wanted to do it with pills. I'm not the violent type. I only wanted to do it gently and be nice to myself. I talked about it twice to where I thought, "Okay, I can get this stuff and I can do it."

As soon as I wrote those notes, the next day, had I still felt the same way, I would have just gone and done it. Over the next day or two, I really made a difference in my mind. I thought, "Nobody has an answer for you. Nobody knows." Because of going to therapy for so long, I was beginning to realize that. I thought, "If you're gonna stay, you're gonna stay and you're not going to feel this bad anymore. You're just not." So I decided—since I thought that closely about dying two times, but I never really acted on it.

I'd been abandoned as a child, my husband had died, big heavy duty things, and every single time, no matter what, I got up, and went on. And I went on farther and faster than most people did anyway. So I thought, "Let's start getting up faster." And it just turned, from that point on. I decided that I could have whatever reasons for living that I wanted at any time. The fact that I made it up, made it more valuable.

What did other people do to help you?

People told me to watch that movie *It's a Wonderful Life*. [laughs] I said, "Give me a break." I don't remember anybody doing anything. Pretty much, I remember getting through it alone. I remember people being enormously uncomfortable when I talked about wanting to kill myself. I'd say, "I can't stand it, I want to die." and they'd say, "Oh, you shouldn't feel like that," and I'd say, "Gee, I do."

I already knew that people couldn't deal with death from my experience with my first husband's illness and death.

People would come into the house, and they'd need help. I would comfort them. My second husband didn't have much to say. And my mother and father—did they have anything to say? No. I asked one friend why she was alive and she said, "Oh, I like to do this," and asked another who said, "I like to do this."

The answers were fine, they were their answers. They have said to me since, that at that time, they had never reached any kind of bottom themselves. So they were giving the kind of group answers anybody who hadn't been pushed to the wall would give. Before my husband's cancer, death, and my tumor, not many bad things had happened in my life—that's why I was so overwhelmed.

When I was suicidal, I wasn't really in a place to be looking for help from other people. I didn't think they could give it. I remember the boyfriend I had after my husband died saying to get professional therapy and my second husband saying the same thing.

What do you wish people had done?
I don't know what I'd want them to do. I only know bad behavior. I don't know good behavior. I can tell you definitely what didn't work. That is, people being unwilling or unable to make themselves emotionally vulnerable. That means they couldn't talk to me. They don't like to see people cry. I think what was good for me was to have the room to just be in that bad place for a while. Because I wasn't out there with a gun, the thinking about it was really good.

How is your life now?
Now I don't really think about suicide. Sometimes I can feel I'm getting really overwhelmed because I have that same feeling that I'm back in that room. But I know what the feeling is, and so I stop it. Nothing's really changed, I just feel better. Even when I feel bad, I feel better. That, to me is just completely changed. I don't think there's any danger (of suicide).

Do you think you emerged a stronger person?
I'd like to say I've emerged a different person. I love what Paul Newman said about his marriage to Joanne Woodward.

He said, "It's just like a toaster. It's been fixed a lot of times. It's not a new toaster."

I'm glad, since I'm living a whole different way. I don't feel lucky, like I saved myself from myself. I don't go around saying, "Thank God." Except once, when I went scuba diving, which was the most incredible thing I've ever done in my entire life. I think, knowing that it was so incredible now, I can say, "God, I wouldn't have missed that for anything." But at that time, I wouldn't have known. I remember being underwater going, "I'm so glad I'm alive to see this." I think it had a lot to do with conquering my own fear. I was never so terrified as when learning how to do that.

It's great to be in love, it's great to have money, it's great to do all these things. And there are rewards (in) the process of going through it. Just seeing yourself go by problems you never used to go by. All of that is sort of interesting. Watching yourself let go of things you think are unjust and not right. You learn something about maturity. I'm having a great time with it. I think this story is a real testimony to therapy. Somebody's willingness to go through and try to figure it out.

How long were you in therapy?
Four or five years, off and on. I'd take six months off when work kept me out of town. During that time, I played golf.

Are you going to stay in therapy?
I don't know. I view therapists like I do exercise class. At the beginning of exercise class, you go there because your body is disgusting. You go there for major work. And then you go to exercise class regularly in order to keep fit. That's how I see it for my brain. I find that I go not nearly as diligently as before because I have a lot of information. I finally learned it. But, I think it's really interesting because it's constantly challenging your notions of what you think is real based on your life as you've lived it. I think it's fascinating.

Any advice for someone who's going through this with another person?
I would send them to professional help immediately. I think it's useless for friends to sit around and go, "Oh you're

fine." I mean, you can be loving.

Were you on antidepressants?
No. In fact, my therapist offered them to me, but I turned them down. I have such a fear of prescription medicine, it's unbelievable. She offered them to me several times because I was enormously depressed, but I just said no. It'd get worse when my weight was up because I wasn't exercising, but when I was exercising, I was always in a better place. A lot of times I took care because I knew not to put myself in jeopardy.

How do you feel about yourself now?
I think that I'm really okay. Despite the psychosis and neurosis that operates in my life all the time—you know, "Have I disappointed anyone?"—I have real knowledge about what it is now. I have real understanding that I'm not perfect, and that the things that are bad about me are just as wonderful as the things that are good about me. If they irritate some people, what am I supposed to do?

What are your plans now?
Right now, I want to go to vet school. That's fine as long as it lasts. If it doesn't last, I'm going to be in that space where I'm kind of free-floating and it feels really dangerous because I don't know why I'm hanging on. I can deal with that. I didn't die in that space of not knowing what was going to happen. Nothing terrible happened to me. I decided if I studied psychology, people would be saying, "Oh yeah, we expected that of you." I just couldn't do it. I may end up there, I don't know.

So you're rebelling?
Rebelling, yeah. I was talking to an advertising art director who gives out jobs and she thinks that no matter when she's around people, they're there to get something. I said, "Well, when you're selling, you're always afraid people are there just to take something."

So I'm going to be dispensing medicine. I'm going to the opposite end, of being a giver. Somewhere in the middle, I'll get a balance.

Greg's Story

Greg is Ellen's brother. He felt a great deal of pressure to succeed in the highly competitive atmosphere of graduate school. There, he met another student who exploited and manipulated him and others in order to succeed. When he seemed to be getting away with it, Greg's ideals and sense of how the world should work were turned upside down. He began to doubt he wanted to continue living. He sought professional therapy and came to a peace with the world. He is now teaching at a university and travels extensively.

How did you come to be suicidal?
Life.

Can you be more specific?
I had thoughts about suicide from the time I was very young. Junior high school, let's say. Maybe before that. But I'm almost thirty-two so let's say, at least twenty years. And it was never, "I want to die." In fact, even recently, it's never, "I want to die." It's, "Stop the world, I want off." It's a different kind of notion. It's, "I don't want to ever have lived."

I want to be dead, but I want everyone to never have had any consciousness of my having lived. The problem with killing yourself is that you cause other people all kinds of pain and doubt and frustration and horrible things. And killing myself has nothing to do with any of that.

I don't want to get their attention. I don't want to say, "Na na na na na." What I want to say is, "I don't want to be here anymore. That's it. I'm gone, poof. I never existed." Minds are erased, memories are erased, all evidence of me is erased just like that. And the difference is a significant one, I think.

This most recent, most serious time, the process that led me to think in suicidal terms was what I would call highly rational. I wasn't particularly lonely. I wasn't particularly depressed. I wasn't particularly frustrated in general about the little minutia of life.

What I was upset about was that the world did not work the way it was supposed to, based on all the things I'd been taught. Therefore, the way in which I was behaving was not functionally useful. The way I was behaving was based on some sense that the world worked in a certain way. I became suicidal.

The world was not a just, fair, good, and proper place. It wasn't well-ordered, it wasn't rational, it was not gentlemanly in the sense of being well-mannered. It was unjust. People who were evil did not get wiped out. People who were good did not get rewarded. While intellectually I'd always known that, it was the first time that it had ever struck me emotionally. I had come to the intellectual conclusion that that was true. I now had a person and a series of events that proved it.

What was that event and that person?
The person is, I think, sociopathic. He will get everything he can from someone, then divorce himself absolutely from that person. If he has to hurt the other person, he'll do that as well. He seems to have no regrets, no problems. Rationalizes the whole process and goes on to the next person.

Is this a friend of yours?
He was. But it wasn't just me he did this to. It was a whole series of people that I introduced him to that gave him incredible advantages. He has consistently screwed over every one of those people in ways that absolutely astonish me. Two of the people have gone into therapy because of this guy. One person stopped his research. A third person almost gave up academics.

And you contemplated suicide?
Yes. At first I was hurt because he'd done that to me. But I realized that he was doing it to everybody, so it wasn't personal anymore, and wasn't going to hurt me. What it meant, though, was that this guy was winning and leaving behind him a trail of shattered lives. It meant nothing to him. And he was winning. You could screw anybody you wanted and win, if you were just good at it. So nothing fit legitimately and therefore, I either had to behave like he did or choose to

not have those goodies at the speed he was getting them. It meant that the world didn't work the way it was supposed to. Altruism did not pay.

That began the suicide process. I sort of dismissed it because I was going off to graduate school. But that, combined with the intensity of graduate school, made me feel inhuman and ugly and stupid and rotten. I'm never going to make it and there's no light at the end of the tunnel. This isn't worth it. I'm going to kill myself. I'm history.

Did you have a plan?

I acquired enough Quaaludes. Quaaludes aren't on the market anymore, but I knew these guys who were South American and they went home and got them for me. Not knowing, of course, that I was going to use them to kill myself. So it would have been very nice, very simple. I would have gone to sleep and it would have been fine. I went through the whole thing of worrying about my family, what they were going to think, and I thought, "Okay, I don't owe anyone any explanations. The world's not the way it's supposed to work. Fine. I'm leaving. Goodbye."

You didn't discuss it with the friends who gave you the drugs?

No. I don't even know if I wanted to do it. I think what I wanted was the freedom to do it. To know that I could, in fact, have enough control over my life that I could take it.

So it was like a safety blanket to have the Quaaludes with you?

Not a safety blanket. It's "I control my world." I got that guy to go get those drugs for me. I now have the ability to kill myself quietly and nobody will know. I even had the foresight to destroy the container. I smashed it up, and I put the drugs in another container that was my own. All that kind of stuff, so that nobody would know about anyone else's involvement.

What stopped you from taking the drugs?

I'm laying in bed a couple of nights before I decide to do this and I think to myself, "I don't have to do this. I can just leave. I don't have to stay in graduate school. Why kill myself when there are other options? What other options are there?" I went through all that corporate world—this kind of job, that kind of job. Seeing all the people I knew. And I finally thought, "Hey, I can get my visas and just travel. Go around the world, go anywhere I want." In fact, I'd be completely locked out of every aspect of my life: my family, my school, my friends, everything, and be okay.

So you figured out options other than suicide?
The minute I decided that, I didn't want to kill myself anymore. It was like, hey, if you've got that, you've got this. All I needed was the sense that I don't have to play that game anymore. I ranted a litany of all the worse-case scenarios I could think of and it ended up being okay. I'd survive. From that moment on, graduate school was extremely easy. I did what I wanted to, when I wanted to do it. I started getting incredible accolades from faculty. People were saying things like, "You seem so relaxed." Or, "You've been so productive." Everything good started happening and I realized that I was recreating the world only because I'd redefined how those peoples' pressures affected me. My world instantly became a better place.

How do you feel now?
I may feel suicidal again, but I really feel like now, the weapon I have against thinking about killing myself is that I can always do something else. There are always other options. People say that all the time, but I don't think they can legitimately believe that until they come to that conclusion themselves.

Some counselors say, "There are other options." But I don't think that does the trick. Now, if the counselor could get that person to somehow run through the litany of options, that might work. So that the person creates the options for himself.

At school, I was a residence hall counselor and director of residence halls. I've had to do things like counsel people not to commit suicide. I know that stuff inside and out. But it wasn't real to me ever, until it was applied to me in my life. I don't think somebody just gives somebody else the answers.

Are you in therapy?
I've been in therapy two years now. He's non-directive. He doesn't give me pat answers. He just talks to me, and we talk back and forth. He finds the patterns, which is what I want. But I'm not feeling healthier. I'm not feeling any more together, any more mature. I don't feel brilliant. I don't feel sophisticated. I don't feel competent.

What are your goals for therapy?
I would like to not be an ass. I would like to be less intense. I would like to be gentle. I would like to be sweet and tall and thin. All those things that somehow I've created as an ideal. What I've decided is, if I could just be stable enough to not wreck friendships, and neurotic enough to be successful, I'll be happy. That's good. That's fine.

So you think you'll be okay?
I accomplish it somehow, despite all my worst fears. What I have to do then, is bring my fears into line. I just have to say, "You have all these experiences that say you're successful, you're competent, you're capable, you're wonderful. Believe that. Forget all that other crap."
I've come to this semi-hostile, semi-relaxed agreement that I'm going to figure out a way to win. I'm going to do it with an all-screwed-up world. And I'm going to do it without violating the people I care about.

Chip's Story

Chip was an active, athletic eighteen-year-old until he became a quadriplegic as the result of an automobile accident. He felt suicidal at the rehabilitation center following the accident and attempted suicide after returning home and seeing the effect his accident had on his family. He was rescued and spent time at a psychiatric hospital. There, he discovered that by helping others with their problems, he took his mind off his own. Chip is working hard to become more independent and has many goals. At the time of this interview, he was writing a book about his experiences.

What is the extent of your disability?

I have a broken neck. I didn't sever my spinal cord. I bruised it. The swelling is what caused my damage. I have fairly good sensation all the way through my body, in my lower extremities, and I have good arm movement. Some of the other spinal cord patients at (my) same level, can't move their arms at all.

I've seen some people at my level who can walk. I always have a problem with that, because I never could understand what's the difference. I've seen people who would be lazy. I never could understand that, either. People who could use their hands but wouldn't walk with leg braces.

I always said, "I wouldn't care if it would take me thirty minutes to walk across the room. I would do it." If I ever can, I will. But they discourage you from that because it's not, how they put it, "functional." Mentally, I think it is very functional. It would help.

Why do they try to discourage you from it?

I have enough arm movement I think, to get to where I could walk with leg braces. But they discourage you from that because it's not functional for everyday use. If it takes me thirty minutes to get from here to there, that's not very practical, they say. But people who say that are up, walking around. I always had a problem with people saying that, or "I know how you feel." That would turn me off quicker than anything.

How did you become disabled?

I'd just turned eighteen. One night, a friend and I met some friends at a restaurant. On the way home, we traveled down a road that has a "dead man's curve" sort of thing. As we came into the curve, my friend thought he was going to hit a rock and he jerked the steering wheel. It sent the car veering to the left and off into the river.

The river was covered with ice and the car rolled down the bank. I was all right through the wreck. The car rolled one more time and the roof hit a rock that was sticking up through the ice. Since I was so tall, it kind of compacted and broke my neck.

I thought I had broken my shoulder. My first thought was, "I've got to get out of the car," because I heard water coming in. The driver helped me keep my head up. I was conscious throughout the wreck, until I got into the ambulance. When I came to, I was in the emergency room.

When did they tell you the extent of the damage?
The day after. When I came to, my parents were there. It was the doctor's son that I had wrecked with. I couldn't figure out why everybody was so upset. I said, "I can't stay in the hospital long because I have a basketball game."

You played basketball?
Basketball, soccer, and baseball. I was very athletic—that was the thing for me. I could have been a good student, but I wasn't. I took real good care of my body. The doctor came in and said, "You've broken your neck." Right away, I assumed that it can't be, because you watch these old western movies and if you break your neck, you die.

Then I started back again with, "How long am I going to be here? I have to play." And he said, "Well..." He couldn't tell me, so he left the room. My mother came in and said that I wouldn't be able to walk. I just assumed it was for a short period, and said, "For how long?" And nobody could really tell me. I eventually found out, but it was kind of a mental block. It just didn't register.

What happened when it began to sink in?
That's kind of a loaded question because psychologically, I don't think I ever accepted the fact that I wouldn't walk. I just learned to deal with it to where I can accept the disability. You have to. With the research and stuff they're doing, I feel if you ever give up and say, "I can't walk and never will again," then you'll lose hope. I never have. I've just simply accepted it to the point to where I can deal with everyday life now.

When did you first become suicidal?
When I was in the hospital, I had an attitude that if I wasn't

going to walk, I wasn't going to do anything. That was it. First of all, I'd never dealt with death that much—I had a couple grandparents die within a two-week period.

Then when I got in here, they put me in a room with a man that had brain cancer. His wife said, "He's going to die, but don't tell him." I was eighteen and I was having enough trouble dealing with what I was going through, without knowing that this man was going to die. I had to sit through every day and watch him.

Plus, the hospital's full of little kids—muscular dystrophy and stuff like that—and several of them died. That's why I couldn't find any logic to religion. There's always the big "why" question. I mean, what good is it? You can't walk, not to mention all the other problems that you have with the injury. I just couldn't understand the point of going on.

Did you go through a period of time when you sat around contemplating all the things you had lost?
About every day. Especially when I'd see somebody on TV in a wheelchair who'd get up and walk, be cured. The soap operas got on a big kick about that. Everybody would be in a wheelchair one week, and the next week they'd try real hard and they're up walking.

The thing that bothered me the most was not really the fact that—well, the fact that I lost my legs is pretty bad—but the fact that I'd missed the time with my brother and sister. That bothered me. Also, you lose your high school associates. They come around for a while, then gradually they don't. I felt like I had matured years above (them). I had a really hard time confiding in people.

I went through several states when I was in the rehabilitation center where I didn't trust people. I confided my thoughts of suicide and felt betrayed. I met a therapist that I confided in that I had suicidal thoughts and didn't feel like life was going to be worth it. I even bought drugs from somebody, but ended up giving them to somebody else to get rid of. The depression was that great.

They had a program called "music therapy." I had confided in this woman and she had come out in the hall and

The Suicide Dilemma

started talking to the psychologist. And, I knew without her saying a word, what she was doing. Sure enough, that night, the staff got into a big—kind of "suicide watch" thing. I decided from that point on, any thoughts I had of trying to do that would be kept to myself.

What happened when you finally got out of the rehab center?

I went to my parents' house. That was okay for a while. I had a real hard time dealing with family because when I was in the hospital, my brother was thirteen or fourteen—my sister was fifteen. I stayed at the hospital for sixty days and the rehab center about nine months. So I missed the time in their lives when they go from being a kid to being an adult. I never, ever have gotten over that, because I missed it because of an accident I had nothing to do with. It's always hurt real bad.

What about the rest of the family? Did they get depressed?

Yeah, my mother was, at times. Things got to be extremely hard on her. I don't think she was getting the help that she needed. I think mentally it was finally getting to her. I was always depressed. I might be a little less depressed one day, but I was always in a depressed state. As far as the rest of the family, I couldn't tell if they were depressed. I wasn't around them as much because they were still in school. But I noticed it in her. That was one of the things that I felt I couldn't deal with.

Could you talk about this with your family?

My family was one of those that... kind of like sex, you know it's there, but you don't talk about it. We're just not an emotional family. There's a lot of things my stepfather doesn't deal with. He may deal with them in his own way. Even at funerals, he is a very private person. As far as helping me get dressed, he wouldn't do it. I don't know if he couldn't. I don't know what his thoughts were. We never discussed it. But he does treat me like a person and not a disabled person. He always has, though. Nothing's changed.

Did you have much contact with your natural father?
No. He had alcoholic problems and I didn't see him for like six months after I broke my neck. I don't know if this is relevant—my real dad's dad shot his wife (my grandmother), then committed suicide. So I always wondered if suicide is hereditary.

That was long before I was born, but that always stuck in my mind. "Well, if you do it, it's just like the rest of the family, so what's the big deal?" It also made me think, "Was I happy in high school? Was I happy before I broke my neck?" I look back and the answer is, "No, I wasn't." I would never have considered suicide then, I don't think. Home life was okay. Not the "Brady Bunch," but it was okay.

Do you think you were more unhappy than most other teenagers?
Yeah. Because I think I was, even back then, forced to grow up quicker than I should have been. That's why I tried to be popular, because it took my mind off of being unhappy. It was like a Dr. Jekyll/Mr. Hyde sort of thing. Immediately, I would leave school and go to work from three to eleven. Then come home, spend as little time there as possible, and go back to school. I had this attitude, "You can't tell me this," because I didn't have a lot of respect for my stepfather. Because nothing I did was good enough for him, but I knew that it wasn't true. I could work my job and everything would be fine. I had respect for authority and had no problems. So I spent time where I got the respect I thought I needed.

You were unhappy, but it appears that you were coping with it.
Well, I don't think you really have a choice. You have to cope with it one way or the other. Then, after I broke my neck and (with) the other complications, it just became too much. Mainly, I got to where I felt nothing. I just felt mentally numb. Didn't feel any emotions—not angry, not sad, not anything. Numb.

At home, you became suicidal again?
I had been really depressed. I just couldn't picture a life

sitting every day and not accomplishing anything. One day, I noticed my mother sitting outside, and she had just broken down and was crying and I just—I grabbed some Valium. I asked my sister to get me a drink and then thought, "No, if I do something and it happens to me, she'll blame herself."

So I waited, and that afternoon, I took the Valium and went outside. I thought that since they were a muscle relaxant, they put you to sleep. I didn't feel guilty. I felt like everybody would be better off. I certainly felt I would be. For a long time, I had contemplated how it would affect them. I just felt that it'd be better all the way around if I were dead. Since I didn't die in the accident.

What was your state of mind when you made the attempt?

I felt very peaceful. I just thought I'd go to sleep and that'd be it. But I pondered for a long time what would happen. You know, would I go to hell? I just couldn't believe, as bad as things were, or as bad as I thought things were, that I would. Because I don't think God meant things to be like that.

After you took the pills, what happened?

I sat outside about thirty minutes and I don't know why, but my mother must have gone into the kitchen where I kept my medicine and noticed the Valium was gone. She came outside and asked me where it was and I didn't say anything. Right away, she knew, because at the rehab center, they used to watch me to see if I was suicidal. I always resented that because I thought, "If I wanted to do something, it's up to me."

What did she do at that point?

They forced me into the car and we went to the hospital. I didn't help at all. I wouldn't cooperate. I went to the hospital, then to a psychiatric hospital for sixty days. After that, I went to a nursing home for about two weeks, then back home.

How did your family react to the suicide attempt?

They were fairly angry. Which I never really understood. To a certain extent, I did. I think they understood some of it, but I don't think they ever really understood—I don't think they ever will—the amount you lose.

I can't really fault them for not understanding. I think what got me was, they didn't really think I meant to kill myself. I was deadly serious. I meant to do it. I didn't succeed and I learned from it. I didn't do it so that, later on, I could come back and say, "I feel suicidal," and everybody'd jump up and pay attention.

We didn't really discuss it. It was more like, "I'm not coming back home. Things were too hard on you." And they said something about a nursing home that offered therapy, and I said, "Fine, I'm going there." I was, by forty years, the youngest person there.

Was the stay at the psychiatric hospital beneficial?
It wasn't beneficial to me. I'm able to help other people no matter where I'm at. I seemed to find myself doing that while I was there. Other people, but not myself. I knew I was depressed, and I guess that's why I have, more or less, gotten myself intact.

How do you feel about things now?
I think I'm in a state where I can deal with things. I still get depressed, so I have to throw myself into other people's situations. I hear a lot from people who have had bad experiences. I used to think, "Here they are, walking around. Why do they commit suicide? What could possibly be so bad for them? They're walking, so they've got it all." Now I realize it's just not that way. You don't have to be in a wheelchair to be suicidal. That was a big step for me.

How did things go when you went back to your folks' home?
I think I tried to make things better. They didn't tiptoe around me just so I wouldn't get—but I think they were more aware of my moods. I think they watched me. Which I could always tell.

I tried to get more involved in doing things instead of having the monotony of just sitting around day by day. Or just getting up and watching soap operas—getting up means suffering and that's your whole day. I started volunteering and doing other things, anything to help somebody else. I felt that would make me feel like I was doing something worthwhile and had a purpose.

Why did you return to the rehab center?
I had a thing when I was hurt where I refused to dress myself, because it wasn't done the way that I'd done it for eighteen years. They let me get by with it. So I went back and I overcame that. Got my driver's license. I'm more independent. I'm this person who happens to be in a wheelchair and can't walk. I try to stay involved as much as I can. I still find this need for people who need help. I don't know why, but people tell me things they don't tell other people. I feel like it takes my mind off my problems if I'm trying to help somebody else figure out how to deal with their problems.

Do you ever dream about how things were?
I'm not in a chair in my dreams. Never. I get up out of the chair, walk to do whatever I'm doing, then come back and sit down. I've had dreams, and woke up and my legs are tired.

You graduated high school in the hospital— have you done anything else educational?
Not as far as continuing my education. That's what I'm in the process of now. I think you go through stages. I think the first couple of years, you just learn to deal with your body. The next couple of years, you learn to deal with the world. But the first couple of years, you just hide away. You're getting used to what to do with your body.

I think by year four or five or six, the year I'm in, you're tired of sitting around and you're getting bored. You realize that if you don't do something, that you're just not going to make it, mentally or physically. There's just no way you can sit around for twenty, thirty, fifty years. It's kind of like a shot we used to call in basketball, the "do or die." You either do it, or mentally, you go downhill. You can get back to a suicidal state.

Do you mean, accepting things as they are and going from there?

There's a certain level of acceptance you get to—have to get to. If you don't—say you stay in that depressed state—you're not able to accomplish anything.

Do you still hold onto the goal of walking?
I think now I have accepted the chair enough to where I can deal with it in everyday life. I still have hope that research will find a cure one day. I had eighteen years. I can still feel what it's like to walk, so I can't block that out of my mind. For a long time, I would see little (disabled) kids of ten or eleven and think, "At least I had eighteen years and they've had nothing." Then later, I would think, "Why should they go through all that?" and I would get more depressed.

On the whole, you see yourself becoming more independent?
It's almost an obsession, because I feel you have to be. Once you've become totally independent, or as close to it as you can, then you feel as normal as you can. You'll still be in a chair, but at least you'll be able to do things for yourself. You won't have to depend on everybody for every little thing that you need.

What are your goals at this point?
I plan to get a job. I'd like to work with disabled people. I'd like to finish the book, a book that just says, "Hey, I broke my neck and I tried to commit suicide. Things with the family were not perfect. Life is not perfect. But I'm still trying."

Ben's Story

At sixty-eight, Ben was healthy and active. He still worked as a custodian—and unofficial heart and soul—for the local elementary school, a job he'd held for years. The patriarch of a very large family, he'd also been very active at the school and in his church. His world fell apart when he found his wife with another man and she told him she wanted a divorce. He grew so depressed, he attempted suicide. He said he knew it was a mistake all along and has learned to accept the divorce and get on with his life. His greatest joys are his grandchildren.

How long ago did you try to kill yourself?
About three years ago.

How old are you now?
Seventy-one. Just retired this year.

What led up to your feeling suicidal?
It started back when I found my wife with someone else, and it just kept leading on. I couldn't tell anybody else. Couldn't talk to her. When she came to me for a divorce, I didn't want to give it to her. But, she just kept on, so I gave it to her. After I'd done that, I said, "Well, I've got nothing to live for, so I'll just take my life and get myself out of the way." I was talking to my mother-in-law about it and she told me, "It isn't worth it." But that didn't stop me from doing it, you know. I became depressed because I knew I was breaking my vow, and that's what was dragging me down. They'd said, "What's joined together, let no man put asunder." So I felt like I had nothing to live for. There was just me. I didn't see how to look at the bright side. But I advise anybody, before they try suicide, to think twice.

Were you feeling like nobody cared?
I just felt like everybody was down on me. I just felt like everybody'd turned their backs on me in the family.

Is there anything your children could have done or said to have stopped you?
No. There wasn't anything anybody could have said that would have stopped me, because I had made my mind up. I'd talked to my mother-in-law and she said I shouldn't do it, but I didn't listen. That's one thing. I always listen to what she has to say, but not that one time.

So you made up your mind to kill yourself?
I went to town, got groceries, came on back, picked up

the telephone, and called one of the kids and told him what I was going to do. He didn't believe me, you know. I told him where he'd find me and everything. I picked up my gun, and the whole time I was going down there, the Lord was telling me not to do it. And the devil was saying, "Go ahead and do it." I paid attention to the devil. Had I paid attention to the Lord, I wouldn't have done it. So my sons pulled into the yard, and I had the gun up to my chest and I pulled the trigger. Just missed my heart.

Luckily, for you.
They didn't remove the bullet. It's too close to my spine. I was in (the hospital) for about three months. On top of that, I had a heart attack. When they were wheeling me on that little thing down the hall, the doctor said, "This man's dying." I said, "Doc, I know it." They were still hitting me with something, some kind of electric shock. I raised up and fell back. The third time, my breath left me. They said they worked on me five or ten minutes. I saw heaven open up, and I saw hell, plain as daylight.

You went through one of those afterlife kind of experiences?
Oh, yeah. They brought me back. I got by, but the next person who might try it, they might die. I advise nobody to do it.

At the time, do you think you were thinking clearly?
No, you're not thinking right. You haven't got your head on straight. You're letting all kind of thoughts run around up there. I had a lot of folks ask me, "So you turned the gun on yourself? Why didn't you shoot them (his wife and her lover)?" I said, "I made a promise to my mother-in-law that before I would harm a hair on their heads, I'd take my own life." That's what I told her last time we talked.

Were you angry?
No, I wasn't angry, I'd just become depressed. Just kept telling myself that I was tired of living. Over and over. My conscience was telling me not to do it, but I just kept repeating

that. If I'd used the right kind of gun, I would have been gone. I carried my shotgun and my pistol, and I used my pistol. I couldn't get the shotgun up in the position to pull the trigger.

It didn't take long for me to realize I'd made a mistake. In fact, I'd known I'd made a mistake before I'd even done it. But, you see, I wouldn't listen to my conscience. My mind was just as good when I'd done that as it is today. I know there's nothing wrong with my mind. But like I said, you get depressed. You don't know what you do till it's too late and when it's done, you can see your mistake. If you're lucky enough to get over it, you can appreciate good health. I knew I was making a mistake before I ever pulled the trigger.

So you were in the hospital three months? Then what?

I came back here (to my son's). The doctor heard the psychologist say, "Isn't a thing wrong with this man's mind." That man had good sense.

You were just depressed?

Yeah. The doctor said he was going to sign me over (to the psychiatric hospital). Then the psychologist said, "You sign that man over there, they'll just be taking his money. There's nothing wrong with this man's mind."

When you were recuperating, you went back to work?

Oh yeah, and I worked up till I got ready to retire. I had two operations since then—hernia and gall bladder.

If you were to go through this again, what would you have done instead of trying to kill yourself?

I'd have just walked on my way. I wouldn't have done it. I'd just say, "Forget about it. If you want somebody else, just go ahead and get him." It's not worth it to me. I'd do it all different.

Would you have talked to your kids or other people more?

Yeah. My mother-in-law is about the only one I talk with. We talk about a million things. She and I talk about what's right and what's wrong. She knows what's going on. Lots of things she knows that I didn't know.

When you realized you were going to live, were you glad about it?
Oh, yeah. I thank the Lord every night when I lay down that he spared me. I had lots to live for. I was thankful I still had my family and friends. I was able to get up and get about and take care of myself. You can get depressed. You won't think about all you've done till it's over with. It's too late then. I'd seen the mistake, but it was too late. I got myself in a worse fix. Suicide doesn't help a bit. I advise anybody not to try to take their life.

Peter's Story

Peter was a thirty-year-old interior designer when he was diagnosed with Acquired Immune Deficiency Syndrome (AIDS). [This interview took place a number of years ago, at a time when there were few treatment options and AIDS was ravaging the gay community in the United States.]
When the disease first flared up and he landed in the hospital, Peter felt suicidal. In the process of preparing for suicide (finding a source for pills with which to overdose, saying his goodbyes, making a will), he rediscovered his passion for life. He learned about dying with dignity by watching the experience of his dying lover. Without discounting the pain, Peter realized he did not want to cut his life any shorter by suicide.

How did having AIDS change your life?
Design meant nothing to me. I felt like I wasn't contributing anything to my life or to anyone else's life. It was very difficult to sit down with a client and discuss for two hours whether a damask or a stripe goes on a dining room chair. She couldn't make up her mind. And I thought, "My God, I

don't have much time left. I've blown an evening doing such a frivolous, stupid thing." I blew up at the client. It was that exact instance.

At that point, I knew, "Okay Peter, you need to get out of this. This is not an effective way to live your life." So I had a wonderful opportunity with my current employer. He hired me knowing I had AIDS, knowing that I would probably have to take time off to get to doctors. He agreed to very flexible hours and salary, so I'm guaranteed an income every month.

What were the circumstances involved in your becoming suicidal?

I think anyone that's diagnosed with a terminal illness goes through deep depression. They have to sort out what they want to do for the rest of their lives. When I was initially diagnosed with KS (Kaposi's sarcoma), because that doesn't hurt and it's not debilitating—it was almost like having acne—it was no big deal, even though it was a confirmed AIDS diagnosis. So I could live with that for a while.

Three months after that, I got PCP (pneumocystis pneumonia). Now, that hurts. My lover had spent a month in the hospital. I was going through the trauma of, "I have AIDS," then a month and a half later, it was, "Mark has AIDS and is very sick." And the day that he was coming out (of the hospital), I was going in. I was losing control of everything in my life—over my own health, over the health of the person I loved. All of our dreams and aspirations as a couple had been shattered because we were unsure of whether or not we'd be around to enjoy a future together.

So, my dreams, my hopes, my health, my love, my spirituality, my emotions—everything was in complete turmoil. Mark and I were both trying to grasp at whatever we could to create some normalcy in our lives, but it just seemed like wave after wave would bring us down.

I was also worried about how I was going to pay the mortgage if I was laid up in a hospital. Who was going to pay the hospital bills? So there was an out of control feeling about the basic necessities of life. How am I going to feed myself? How am I going to house myself? I was out of control with my relatives. What do you tell your relatives?

Did they know that you're gay?

My immediate family knew. It had never been discussed with my grandmothers or my extended family. I come from a very large family and we're very tight. We love each other dearly. So I had to think, "What if they don't respond the way I want them to? What if they don't reach out with love?"

I spent the next month in the hospital. The day after Thanksgiving, I went in, so it meant spending Christmas in the hospital. People brought in little Christmas trees and were real sweet, but I thought, "This is my last Christmas. And I'm not enjoying it because I can't breathe. I don't feel good."

I was concerned about all of the emotional turmoil that was going on around me. Having people hold my hand and cry. That's very disturbing, because it's bringing to light how seriously sick you are. It's not like a gall bladder operation, and they bring in flowers and say, "Talk to you when you get home." There's a chance that I wasn't ever coming home again.

All of those thoughts ran through my mind when I was awake. I was playing the "what if" game. What if I die? What if I survive this and I'm not able to work and generate an income? What if my relatives abandon me or treat me differently? What if, what if, what if? I was driving myself nuts in the process. I have since learned we don't have a lot of control over our futures. All we have is the moment.

I went to my folks' house and they were all over me. "Are you hungry? Are you cold? Do you hurt? Do you have diarrhea?" Real personal involvement and I wasn't used to that. I've been very independent since I was nineteen. So there was a conflict between recognizing that they wanted to love and be close to me, unlike they had ever been close to me before. Yet, at the same time, I was very uncomfortable. I wanted to say, "Leave me alone." But I recognized their need to love me.

So there was a lot of stress because I was performing for them and I wasn't fully thinking of myself, because I thought that would be selfish. I've since realized that they have to be responsible for what they think and do and feel, and I have to be responsible for me. We need to be honest and say, "I don't like that right now."

The Suicide Dilemma

After about two weeks of being with my folks, I came back home and was well enough that I thought that I could function on my own. I tried to go back to Mark, but at that point, he had felt abandoned by me because I didn't come home to him, I went to my folks' house. Of course, Mark was having his own emotional upheaval and this just added insult to injury. I did everything I could. But he just didn't want to have anything to do with me. He was hurting so much, not only for himself, but for me. It was very painful when we saw each other in the hospital, to see the other one so confused and hurting on every single level.

At that point, all I could do was stare at the carpet. That's all I remember for two weeks. Sitting on the sofa, staring at the carpet. There were a couple of nights that I didn't go to bed. I would be aware that the sun was going down because of the light in the apartment, but that's all my awareness was. I think I was insulating myself from all of the pain I was feeling. I found comfort sitting on the sofa, staring at the carpet fibers. It meant nothing. I was disassociating myself from everything in my physical world. I was trying to get to nothingness. It was a horrendous process to get my brain to stop thinking about AIDS, my mortality, Mark's mortality, everyone's mortality, my folks' tears, the hurt. All I could see was vast pain.

After a while I thought, if I'm going sit here for the rest of my life, trying to disassociate myself from life, that didn't make any sense to me at all. In fact, that was just as painful as living life at that point. So I thought, "It makes sense to kill yourself, and in that process, gain a bit of control of life." That was the one thing that I could do—get an immediate response and be free of all of this insanity.

I have a roommate, a dear girl, and she's helped me out and been totally supportive through this. I thought, "Well, you can slit your wrists, or you can get a gun and shoot yourself, but where are you going to do it?" I started thinking about my roommate. Wouldn't that be horrendous if she walked in and saw the mess in the home that we created? I couldn't do that to her. I thought, "I wouldn't want anybody to do that to me."

The next thing would be to go outside the home and do it, but if a perfect stranger ran across someone who's blown his brains out, I'm sure that scars him for life, and I don't want to do that to anyone. Then, I thought, "Drugs are good. I could just fall asleep and it would be very peaceful and someone would discover my body somewhere, go through that whole horrendous experience." It's scary. Our society doesn't deal with death very well. I don't think we fully acknowledge the process of death.

Anyway, I decided that I would get drugs. I didn't know any drug dealers, and I thought, "What you've got to do is get some things in order so you can die. Make a will." I hadn't really taken care of myself—hadn't shaved, hadn't done anything for several days—and I thought, "I've got to get myself pulled together before I get in my car or get on the phone, or whatever I have to do to get these drugs."

In the process of cleaning myself up—and looking in the mirror and going, "You know, it's not too bad. You managed to pull that together," and making the bed and preparing meals—I started to accept calls. Talking to people, and their expressions of concern and love, kind of turned me around. At that point, I was recovering from the pneumocystis to where I was feeling better every day.

People would ask me out for dinner and I thought, "Well, that will be our last dinner. We'll acknowledge that this will be the final thing, and I can say my goodbyes." Well, we laughed and had fun, and I realized how really dear those people were and that I wanted a lot more nights with them.

I rediscovered the process of living and loving, not only other people, but myself. I gained a new respect for life. I rediscovered what life is about. My perspectives changed from one of "Life is horrible and painful and hurts too much" to one of "Life can be pretty damn good if you seek out those people and loved ones that will support you in it."

Any more thoughts about suicide?
About three months after that bout with pneumocystis, we were talking about suicide in my support group and one of the guys took me aside afterwards and said, "I want to have a suicide kit in my home for the reasons we talked about—control. I want to be able to stop it when it gets too much."

So we went down to Mexico one Saturday and the Mexican government, just two months prior, had pulled (the drug we wanted) from the pharmacy shelves. We were real disappointed that we weren't able to get it. Instead, I bought another drug which isn't quite as sure-fire. I have it and suppose if I really feel the need to make use of it, at least I know it's there.

Are you actually planning that when things get really bad...

No, it's just a pacifier. I don't think I'll use it. Mark's dying right now. Even if he wanted to commit suicide at this point, he is so debilitated—and his mind is off—he couldn't do it. That's the rotten thing about suicide. How do you determine that this is it? When do you know that this is the last moment? I think a lot of people hang on to hope. I've seen it with persons with AIDS. We've had discussions about dying. Mark knows he's dying. We've talked about what is beyond, and he's not frightened.

What that is teaching me is that there really is no need for suicide. The pain that he is enduring... he's showing me that it's okay to die and that the death process doesn't have to be an ugly, lonely, heartbreaking, horrible experience. He and his friends and relatives are showing me that it has everything to do with love and support, which is what I think life is all about. I'm really grateful to be by his side and see all the love that is pouring in. I want that. I wouldn't want to deprive anyone of that experience. I can't kill myself. I need my friends' and family's love. I need to help them resolve my death.

From what you're going through with Mark, you know what they need.

Yeah. I certainly don't want to inflict pain or hurt or sadness on anyone. I know that by committing suicide, I would just be speeding up the process. Life is going much too fast for me to speed anything up. I'm on a completely different timetable now that I have AIDS. I feel like in the last two years, I've rushed through about thirty years.

I remember within the first year or so, I went through something like a midlife crisis where I wanted a sports car. I wanted to have an affair—I don't know who I'd have an affair with, but you know the thought, "I want to grab some lustful, wild fantasy just one last time." I calmed down from that and now I guess my thoughts are more like a geriatric might think, "God, I can't believe things have changed so much. Everything's going so fast." I look at my nieces and nephews and I think, "Wow, they've grown so quickly."

My time is so precious to me, I really evaluate how I want to spend it, and I'm having to learn to say no to a lot of things. I want every moment to be quality. I'm going to spend it with the people that I really love or people that I really care about, or that I can help. That's my big thing right now. We've got to learn some lessons from this whole process.

The government is not... I don't know what they're doing. The AIDS community has been told very clearly, "You don't count." Acknowledging my homosexuality was a very strange experience because I had always been taught that it was wrong. So I had a very negative self-image. I had this deep dark secret that I didn't dare tell anybody about. I'm getting that thrown back at me again that I'm different, I'm weird, I'm deviant. A lot of judgment has come back since I've been diagnosed—they're discounting us. That instills in me enough anger that I want to do something about it.

When I'm surrounded by people who love me, that instills hope in me to keep going. It's kind of a nice balance. That's what motivates me, my anger and my hope. People have to get more informed about AIDS, about death and dying, about suicide. I think it won't be as frightening, as awful as our fantasies we create for ourselves.

Have you had friends with AIDS who have committed suicide?

Yes. I was very angry when Jeff committed suicide, and I wasn't given the opportunity to hold his hand and tell him how much I loved him and to get that response back.

What would you have said to Jeff if he'd told you he was suicidal?

I'd want to find out, "Why do you want to do this?" I'd talk about death, and say, "Are you okay with death? You feel that there is nothing after you kill yourself, or that there's a heaven or a hell or some other dimension?" Then I'd want to talk about the people that he would be affecting through suicide. I'd go through the same thing that I went through in my head when I was thinking about it: "Who's going to find your body? Who would you want to find the body?"

I think we might do a little visualization exercise. I could say, "Visualize your mom walking into your room and seeing your body there. See her tears and see her hysteria." Maybe we'd reverse it. "What if it was your mom and you walked in on her? What would you feel?" I think I'd try to walk him through the process through a fantasy world, show just how awful that might be. Then I'd ask, "Are you sure you want to do that? Is your pain greater than the pain you're going to inflict on a whole lot of people? It's not just mom and dad, brother, sister, girlfriend or boyfriend. It's going to mess up a whole lot of people that don't even know you."

I know what pain's about. It does hurt. But, if there's some way that you can get a person to key into the positive aspects of their pain and feed that positive, such as, "I'm hurting. I feel terrible, but look at all the love that's around. Look at Dad crying at the bedside. Isn't that an incredible, loving, wonderful thing?" My dad and mom have never been as close as they are now. It took this experience to bring us to that kind of intimacy. (The suicidal person) needs to get into some supportive environment and drink up all the love that he can. I think he'll rediscover life, and go, "Yeah, this is pretty great. I want more of this."

You're lucky because you've got a lot of support. What would you say to somebody who was on his own? What can he do personally?

It's time that they reach out. If they've been alone for that many years that they don't have any friends or family that respect and admire them, maybe it's time that they reach out to somebody and seek some love and support. Be real honest and say, "I need to be held. I need to be loved. I need my rent paid." Whatever. Unless you're living on an island, there are places for support.

Were you ever suicidal or depressed before?

No. I was very happy. I was very satisfied with life. I was born with a cleft palate. My nose was deformed, so starting two weeks after birth, I had some pretty painful operations—plastic surgery. Every two summers, I'd go into the hospital and I knew what I was in for. It was miserable. It was horrible. Until I was sixteen and old enough and smart enough to go, "Stop! I don't want any more of this. This is crazy." I was satisfied with the way I looked at that point.

But, I remember laying in those hospital beds thinking, "I healed." I would put myself in a fantasy world when the pain got too great. I'd visualize that I was skiing on the lake at my uncle's. I knew that if I could just hold on, I'd be able to do all those fun things again. I could have thought about suicide. "Am I going to keep doing this year after year?" But I never did it. I've had a charmed life. It's still charming.

Do you think your experience as a child steeled you for what you're going through now?
Yes, it did. It gave me some coping mechanisms that I don't think too many people have tapped into. I was very sick as a kid, not just with the cosmetic surgery, but ear infections, throat problems, nose problems. It certainly instilled a fight in me, and a hope. And maybe even a fantasy that I can overcome this. When I was in the hospital, it was a fantasy world that I created. I thought, "I can overcome this."

Maybe I'm still doing that now. I keep thinking, "If I keep working at this, maybe I can overcome AIDS." I can overcome AIDS on several different levels. It's not just a physical process. I know that I have enough control of my mind that I can disassociate myself from the pain when it hurts. Mark is teaching me through his experience that you can disassociate yourself from the drama of that. I think that's a bit different than denial. Denial just flat-out says, "It's not happening." Disassociation acknowledges the experience, but then says, "I'm so much more than this experience."

How have your goals changed since your diagnosis?
I want to help people. I've seen so much pain and hurt, and I'm real tired of it. So it motivates me to get rid of it somehow, whether it's acting in a political vein or educating people so that society is more compassionate and understanding. I guess you can say that my goals have become much

more humanitarian rather than selfish. It would be nice to have a wonderful apartment, but that's not important to me anymore. If I can have 12 hours a day helping people, I'd prefer that to just about anything. This disease is teaching me about love—how to love. That feels great.

Did you seek professional help when you were suicidal?

No, not during that two-week period when I was really attempting to figure out a responsible way to commit suicide—if there is such a thing. I saw somebody when I was first diagnosed, and I went to a psychologist for a few months after that.

Did you feel suicidal when you were diagnosed two years ago?

No. In fact, two weeks before my diagnosis, I went to see my best friend. We were talking about AIDS and he said, "What if you were diagnosed with AIDS?" I remember saying, "I would book a flight to Mexico, get some drugs, walk into the jungle, take the pills and die."

When the diagnosis came through, there was this great need to live. That's all I kept thinking "I've got to live. I've got to pull through this. I'm not going to die. I cannot die. I will not die." My questions to the doctor were, "How am I going to get through this? What can I do?" I was looking for how I could continue life rather than kill myself.

I couldn't fully understand or recognize what it meant to have AIDS at that point because I felt great. It wasn't until later when I came down with pneumocystis and I physically felt the effects of the virus, and I thought, "Okay, this is AIDS."

Even today, I have new KS lesions, I'm going through chemotherapy, but sometimes it doesn't fully sink in what's happening to me. It's strange to get undressed, go by the mirrors, and see how my body's changed. I don't have enough energy to work out anymore, so all of those muscles that I worked so hard for, for so many years, are gone. Another element of losing control.

You often mention control. Would you describe yourself as a perfectionist?
Very high standards, but I don't know about perfectionism. Some of those things came to light when I was thinking about suicide—that I wasn't enough. All of the work that I had done so far was just being taken away from me. Not perfectionism. But not being able to attain the quality of life that I wanted.

I guess it also ties into the changing body image.
Right. That was another thing that I was always striving for—this terrific body. To be as attractive as I possibly could. I wanted a nice house, I wanted a nice car, I wanted everything to be pretty and in its place. And it's always been pretty and in its place. I just didn't recognize it. It took AIDS to help me figure that out. I guess I was striving for a perfection that doesn't exist.

AIDS for me has been a very freeing experience because I've been able to dump all that. It's disturbing to see my body change, but I can still find aspects of it that I like. My physical image has changed completely. My physical goals have changed. How I view people has changed completely. There isn't a person that I run into anymore that I can't find something lovely about, where three years ago, I would have seen their flaws.

Now—because I don't have great skin anymore, I'm losing my hair, my body is deteriorating—I'll just be fascinated looking at them. It's this appreciation for health that carries over into everything in my life. The sky, the plants, the fresh air. Not being able to breathe very well for a month, you establish this new appreciation for breathing.

But when I was suicidal, I didn't care about any of that. It was when I started perceiving it in a positive way—seeing the beauty and love in everything—that I thought, "Well, I think I like life. I'd like to hang onto it a little longer."

Which you don't want to cut any shorter by suicide?
Uh uh. I'm seeing through Mark's death how he's hanging onto those moments that we're all together. It's like, "Wow, this is really great. I'm just not quite ready to let go of this

right now." I hope that's what he's thinking.

You don't support euthanasia or rational suicide?
I'm praying that Mark will die at this point. He isn't even there. I keep thinking, "Just let go. Go on." Maybe part of that's selfish. Part of it is also a lot of love for him. I want him to go on to something better, and at this point, I think death might be more comfortable for him. I don't know. I couldn't do it (suicide) for myself. I don't think I could help Mark.

Have any of your friends asked you to help them commit suicide?
No. I have a good friend who has his suicide kit at home. His last bout—his third—with PCP, we thought we were going to lose him. The drugs they give you are so powerful and so miserable, you really have to question which is worse—the virus and the opportunistic infections, or the drugs. The second week when I was into my treatment, I felt worse than when I went in. I thought, "What am I doing this for? This is incredibly stupid."

When my friend came out of the hospital, he said, "I think that this may be the time to get out the kit." I said, "If you can hold on, just give it ten days without any of these drugs, then we'll talk about the kit. But hold on for that period, because a lot of it is the drugs speaking to you." You feel so awful that, of course, your mind is going to go, "I hate this, I hate my life." It's going to instill all those awful, depressing thoughts. Anyway, he waited the ten days and he was feeling a whole lot better. So I asked him to please tell me that the next time, if the positions are reversed.

Where do you draw the line between euthanasia and suicide?
It's very vague if there is a line. I have a living will that says my parents have the authority to stop medication at any point that they think it's useless. Just to prolong life—I don't think that makes any sense. But where do you draw that line? And at that point, are you all giving up hope? I've seen enough people recover after being on their deathbed and I think, "Well, maybe that isn't the line. Then we should wait." I'm

very optimistic and I keep thinking, even with Mark, "Maybe something will happen."

With AIDS having no cure, what do you say if someone says, "What's the difference if I do it now or wait and go through this possibly horrible process?"

I can only speak from my own experience, which has been very positive. I'm not discounting the horribleness that I've been through. I'm not discounting all the pain. But I also have been open to a new vision in life, which is so much better than the thirty years prior to my diagnosis, I'm willing to take on the pain.

I have done more living in the last two years than I did in the thirty years prior because I opened myself up to the experience of acceptance of people and things around me. Before, I was trying to control and now I don't try to control anything at all. What happens, I'll go with it. That's a wonderful experience, to not have that responsibility of trying to manipulate the world and people and relationships and environments.

All of the people interviewed are glad they didn't kill themselves. Though it was a terrible episode in their lives, each person was able to learn from it. They learned to use new and better coping skills and were able to make positive changes in their lives.

While it may have seemed impossible to them at one time, they've all found things to live for. Hopefully, their self-awareness will help to protect them from considering suicide ever again.

Don't be afraid to try to reach out to a suicidal person. You can help him get through a difficult, but temporary, stage in his life. Suicidal people do not have to die—especially if they have caring significant others around them.

Nine

What Is Most Important to Remember?

The Main Points of This Book

Suicidal Signals to Look For

Situational Clues: Loss of a loved one through death or divorce, economic loss, loss of health, loss of a sense of identity, loss of ideals, loss of a job, or retirement. Be aware of the significance of the loss to that particular person. Pay special attention if the loss is unexpected or several losses happen in succession.

Verbal Clues: Ranging from blatant—"I'm going to kill myself," to subtle—"Nobody needs me anymore." Take any suicidal talk seriously.

Behavioral Clues: Previous suicide attempts, giving away possessions, sudden recovery from depression, buying a gun, writing a suicide note, resigning from clubs and organizations, unexplained changes in behavior patterns.

Symptoms of Depression: Changes in eating, sleeping and hygiene habits, anhedonia, apathy, loss of ability to concentrate, excessive crying, physical illness, loss of sex drive, feelings of worthlessness, consistent pessimism, and irritability.

Stages in Becoming Suicidal

1. The person experiences psychological pain and inner turmoil as a result of a loss.
2. The person's attempts to cope with the situation fail.
3. The person feels helpless and hopeless about himself and his situation. He interprets the world as negative.
4. The person develops "tunnel vision," seeing suicide as the only way out.

Your Positive Allies in Suicide Prevention

Ambivalence: The person doesn't necessarily want to die, he just wants to change his situation. Ambivalence causes him to signal his distress through suicidal behaviors.

Relative Shortness Of Suicidal Crisis: The length of time during which the person is in danger of killing himself is often very short.

How Do I Know if the Person Is Serious?

Stage 1: Calling for Help

The person in question is beginning to feel hopeless regarding his present situation. He is probably experiencing low self-esteem and feeling helpless to make changes. He may be depressed over potential or actual losses, and may have fleeting thoughts of suicide.

Stage 2: Life at Risk

The individual is feeling the same as the people in Stage 1, but with greater intensity. The person is ambivalent about living, and may actually be flirting with death through reckless behavior. He may be experiencing a fairly high level of anxiety and may not be thinking clearly. Believing he has no options other than death, he has begun to make a plan for suicide. This plan raises the risk that he will attempt suicide.

Stage 3: Life at High Risk

The person feels suicide is the only way out. He's got a definite plan for killing himself and is looking for the best time to do it. He may appear completely down and depressed. Or he may suddenly seem happier and less depressed, now that he's made the definite decision to kill himself. Watch for this extreme, sudden change in mood.

Stage 4: Suicide Attempt

The person has made a suicide attempt or suicide gesture.
Call 9-1-1. You may need to take control of the situation in order to save the suicidal person's life.

Always call a mental health professional if you suspect that someone is suicidal. Seek professional guidance in handling these situations.

Talking with the Suicidal Person

1. **Gather your courage and talk to the person.**
   Be positive, supportive, and if necessary, persistent. Tell him why you're concerned.
2. **Listen, listen, listen.**
   You don't need to have all the answers.
3. **Be supportive.**
   Let him know that feeling depressed due to life's stresses and upheavals is normal.
4. **Ask him if he's suicidal.**
   Don't be afraid to ask him right out, "Are you thinking of killing yourself?"
5. **Offer other options.**
   Make some suggestions. Encourage the suicidal person to seek professional help.

6. **Discuss the suicide plan.**
   Find out how dangerous the person is to himself.
7. **Get the person to professional help.**
   Take the initiative. Help the person structure his time until he sees the therapist. Follow through to make sure he gets professional help.

If you don't feel you can talk to the suicidal person yourself, ask another significant other or possibly the suicidal person's doctor or clergyman to go with you, and call a therapist and ask for assistance.

Use "I" statements, such as, "I am worried about you."

Emphasize that you care about the suicidal person.

Keep in touch with the suicidal person until he sees a therapist. Do not leave him alone if you think he's in danger of killing himself.

Get others involved—**including significant others and mental health professionals** as soon as possible.

The most important thing is to *take action.*

Methods of Treating Suicidal People

Antidepressants—Antidepressants may be used to relieve depressive symptoms and help the patient think more clearly, so he can process the psychotherapy better.

Psychotherapy—Psychotherapy helps the patient see other options and learn better coping methods.

Nutrition And Exercise—The mind functions better when the body functions better.

Ten

What if a Person I Care About Kills Himself?

Survivors of Suicide

Despite the best efforts of significant others and mental health professionals, a number of people will kill themselves. Suicide is devastating to everyone left behind. Dealing with a death by suicide is different than dealing with any other kind of death. Family and friends begin a long, agonizing period characterized by intense guilt, anger, and grief. They wonder if others are blaming them. They wonder what to say to relatives, friends, and neighbors. They wonder how to explain it to themselves.

Many survivors of suicide attempt to deal with it by denying the suicide. They say the suicide was actually an accident or they come up with an entirely different explanation for the person's death.

The self-recrimination and guilt can be intense, especially for parents when a child commits suicide. The questions replay in their minds over and over. "What could I have done differently?" "Why didn't I realize what he was planning?" "What did I miss?"

Many people left behind are surprised by their own anger with the dead person. Upon finding her husband's dead body, Teresa kicked the corpse repeatedly and yelled at it. "I screamed, 'How dare you leave me? You'd promised you'd never leave me.' I was angry he left me alone. I'd fought so hard to keep him alive."

Survivors of a suicide find that it affects them for the rest of their lives. A fear develops in many families that another relative will follow in the suicidal person's footsteps or that emotional problems "run in the family." It can affect present and future relationships, destroy marriages, and worsen drinking and drug problems. The cloud of anxiety and uncertainty can affect the family for generations.

Survivors May Need Help Too

"At first I took it personally. If he really loved us, he would have stuck around," says Teresa. "It was a blow to my self-esteem. If a woman's love wasn't enough to keep him alive... I thought to myself, 'You idiot, how much love did you have if you didn't pick up that he was really going to do it?' I hated myself and went through this self-punishment thing through anorexia."

Too many survivors, due to shame and guilt, bottle these feelings inside themselves. This is the reason many families cannot heal after such a tragedy. Often, they are in too much of a hurry to move on with their lives and forget it ever happened. They don't allow themselves to go through the necessary grieving process. The anniversary of the suicide can be especially traumatic for survivors.

Many who have suffered this type of loss find help in support groups and family counseling. In addition to the traditional inpatient and outpatient mental health services, many communities offer support groups for survivors of suicide through churches and other community organizations. You can also contact the American Association of Suicidology to find support groups for survivors of suicide.

It is important that members of the family are not isolated from one another, blaming themselves and wondering how much others are blaming them. Everyone close to the victim should be included: grandparents, aunts, uncles, cousins, and non-relatives who were close friends.

In the case of teenage suicide, schools and family should become actively involved in helping friends and classmates deal with the death. There are numerous websites that will assist teachers and administrators in accessing information to develop intervention programs after a student has committed suicide.

When a youth suicide occurs, the event itself and the grief process should be addressed immediately. The more quickly, openly, and honestly a loss by suicide is dealt with, the less likely there will be a suicide cluster among young people in the community. Follow the same guidelines that you would for setting up a suicide prevention education program, and ask a mental health professional experienced in handling suicides or find another expert on the subject to speak to the school.

Friends and classmates will need help dealing personally with the suicide. Set up a network of mental health professionals, teachers, counselors, coaches, parents, and other students, so that confused or suicidal students know who they can talk to. Again, the most important thing is to be able to give students support as quickly as possible.

The good news is that there is healing. While the suicide may always be with you in some ways, it does not have to dominate the rest of your life.

Selected Bibliography

Alexander-Passe, Neil, "Dyslexia: Investigating Self-Harm and Suicidal Thoughts/Attempts as a Coping Strategy," *Journal of Psychology & Psychotherapy*, 2015 Vol. 5, Issue 6.

Alvarez, Alfred. *The Savage God: A Study of Suicide.* New York: Random House, 1972.

American Foundation for Suicide Prevention, Suicide Statistics, 2016.

Archer, Dale, MD, "White Middle-age Suicide in America Skyrockets," *Psychology Today*, May 6, 2013.

"Bipolar Disorder and the Risk of Suicide," *Everyday Health,* Bipolar Disorder Center, 2018.

Bipolar Lives, "Bipolar Suicides," published online, November 2017.

Bipolar Lives, "Bipolar Suicide Myths, Living Better With Bipolar," published online, April 20, 2018.

Boree, C. George, "Neurotransmitters," *General Pyschology*, 2009.

"Bullying Statistics, Anti-Bullying Help, Facts, and More," *NoBullying.com.* Online, 2018.

"Bullying and Suicide," Substance Abuse and Mental Health Services Administration, *SAMHSA.gov.*, Online, September 20, 2017.

Cain, Albert C., *Survivors of Suicide.* Springfield, IL: Charles C. Thomas, 1972.

Centers for Disease Control and Prevention (CDC) Data and Statistics Fatal Injury Report for 2016.

Cherry, Kendra, "Identifying Neurotransmitters and Brain Health, Different Types and Why They are Important,"

Brain Health, May 10, 2018.

Clayton, Paula J., MD, Professor Emeritus, University of Minnesota School of Medicine, American Foundation for Suicide Prevention, "Suicidal Behavior and Mental Health Disorder," *Mereck Manual,* consumer edition, 2016.

Data and statistics taken from the Centers for Prevention and Control (CDC) 2022.

Dilsaver, Steven C., MD, "Suicide Attempts and Completions in Patients with Bipolar Disorder," *Psychiatric Times*, Volume 24, May 2007.

Elia, Josephine, MD, Professor of Psychiatry, Human Behavior, Kimmel, Sidney, Professor of Pediatrics, Medical College of Thomas Jefferson University: Attending Physician, Nemours, A.J., Dupont Hospital for Children, "Suicidal Behavior in Children and Adolescents," *Mereck Manual,* consumer edition, April 30, 2018.

"Estimating the Risk of Attempted Suicide Among Sexual Minority Youths," *JAMAnetwork.com*. Online, December, 2018.

Gregory, Christine, PhD, "Suicide and Suicide Prevention: understanding the risks factors, prevention and what we can do," *Psycom,* 2018.

Grollman, Earl A. *Suicide: Prevention, Intervention and Postvention.* Boston: Beacon Press, 1971.

Harkavy-Friedman, Jill, PhD, "Learning More About Suicidal Ideation," *nami.org.* (National Alliance on Mental Illness). Online, August, 26, 2017.

Hatton, Corrine L., Valente, Sharon M. and Rink, Alice, *Suicide Assessment and Intervention.* New York: Appleton-Century-Crofts, 1977.

Kennedy-Moore, Ph.d., Eileen, "Suicide in Children - What Every Parent Must Know," *www.psychologytoday.com*, September 24, 2016.

Khazan, Olga, "No, Suicides Don't Rise During the Holidays," *The Atlantic*, 2015.

Klagsbrun, Francine, *Too Young to Die: Youth and Suicide,* New York: Pocket Books, 1984.

Klott, Jack, MSSA, LISW, CSW, *Suicide and Psychological Pain: Prevention That Works*, 2017.

Levinson, Douglas F., MD, Nichols, Walter E., MD, "Genetics and Brain Function," Stanford Medicine: Genetics and Brain Function, 2018.

Los Angeles Times Wire Service, "Girl, 11, Kills Herself Over Cigarette Find," *Los Angeles Times,* April 5, 1985.

Maltsberger, John T. *Suicide Risk: The Formulation of Clinical Judgment,* New York University Press, New York, 1986.

Means Matter, Duration of Suicidal Crises, Harvard T.H. Chan School of Public Health, July 25, 2018.

Miller, Marv, *Introduction to Suicidology,* 1981 and 1988.

Miller, Marv, *Suicide After 60: The Final Alternative,* New York: Springer Publishing Co., 1979.

Miller, Marv, ed., *Suicide Intervention by Nurses,* New York: Springer Publishing Co., 1982.

National Institute of Mental Health, "Understanding the Characteristics of Suicide in Young Children," *www.nimh.nih.gov*, December 14, 2021.

National Veteran Suicide, Veteran Suicide Data: 2016 Update, Online, *mentalhealth.va/gov/suicide_prevention/data.asp.*

Nordqvist, Christian, "What are Suicidal Thoughts?" Reviewed by Timothy J. Legg, PhD, CRNP, *Medical News Today,* July 25, 2018.

Oquendo, Dr. Maria, President of the American Psychiatric Association, "National Institute on Drug Abuse and Advancing Addiction Science," Excerpt from Congressional briefing, April 20, 2017.

Oquendo, Maria A, MD, Galfalvy, Hanga, PhD., Russo, Stefani, BA, Ellis, Steven P., PhD., Grunebaum, Michael F., MD, Burke, Ansley, PhD., and Mann, John, MD., "Prospective Study of Clinical Predictors of Suicidal Acts After a Major Depressive Episode in Patients with Major Depressive Disorder or Bipolar Disorder," *Clinician Manual of Child and Adolescent Psychopharmacology*, Third Edition, 2004.

Oquendo, Dr. Maria, President of the American Psychiatric Association, "Opioid Use Disorders and Suicide: A Hidden Tragedy: National Institute on Drug Abuse," Excerpt from Congressional briefing, 2017.

Pappas, Stephanie, "Suicide Statistics, Warning Signs and Prevention," *Live Science*, August 10, 2017.

Pebody, Roger, National AIDS Manual, *aidsmap.com*, Online, April 6, 2017.

Pescolido, Bernice A. and Georgianna, Sharon, "Durkheim, Suicide, and Religion: Toward A Network Theory Of Suicide," *American Sociological Review,* Vol. 54, No. 1, February, 1989.

Pfeffer, Cynthia R., *The Suicidal Child,* New York: The Guilford Press, 1986.

Price, Michael, "Suicide Among Pre-Adolescents " American Psychological Association, October 2010.

Rodriguez, Tori, MA. LPN PN, "Suicidal Ideation in Bi-polar Depression: A Potential New Treatment," *Psychiatric Advisor,* March 30, 2017.

Rosenfeld, Linda & Prupas, Marilyne, *Left Alive: After A Suicide Death in the Family,* Springfield, IL: Charles C. Thomas, 1984.

Shneidman, Edwin S., "At the Point of No Return," *Psychology Today,* March, 1987.

Shneidman, Edwin S., *Definition of Suicide,* New York: John Wiley & Sons, 1985.

Shneidman, Edwin S., Farberow, Norman L., Litman, Robert E., *Psychology of Suicide,* New York: Science House, 1970.

Shneidman, Edwin S., ed. *Suicidology: Contemporary Developments,* New York: Grune & Stratton, 1976.

Stufflebeam, Robert, "Neurons, Synapses, Action Potentials and Neurotransmission," Consortium on Cognitive Science Instruction, 2008.

Suicidal Thoughts and Behaviors Among U.S. Adults, 2016, SMHSA and The Centers for Disease and Control.

Tishler, Carl L., PhD., "Suicide Behavior in Children Younger than 12: a Diagnostic Challenge for Emergency Personnel," *Academic Emergency Medicine*, 2007.

University of Washington School of Social Work, "Facts About Mental Illness and Suicide," 2018, School of Social Work Mental Health Reporting.

Youth Risk Behavior Surveillance System (YRBSS) published by the Centers for Disease Control and Prevention, 2017.

Rebecca M. Gibson is a Licensed Clinical Social Worker. She has been a mental health clinician since 1976, and has worked in psychiatric hospitals, community mental health centers, and in private practice.

Lynn Mills is a writer, journalist, mother, and ex-race car driver. She lives in Southern California and has a lifelong interest in mental health issues.

www.thesuicidedilemma.com

www.ingramcontent.com/pod-product-compliance
Lightning Source LLC
Chambersburg PA
CBHW030519080526
44586CB00011B/254